The Kings Of Judah And Israel: Or The History Of The Jews

Religious Tract Society

THE

KINGS

OF

JUDAH AND ISRAEL;

OR,

THE HISTORY OF THE JEWS, FROM THE ACCESSION
OF DAVID TO THE BABYLONISH CAPTIVITY.

LONDON:

THE RELIGIOUS TRACT SOCIETY,
Instituted 1799.
SOLD AT THE DEPOSITORY, 56, PATERNOSTER ROW;
AND BY THE BOOKSELLERS.

1837.

LONDON :
Printed by J. Hill, Black Horse Court,
Fleet Street

Sketch of tombs in the valley of Jehoshaphat, where that monarch is supposed to be buried.

INDEX OF REIGNS.

A
CHRONOLOGICAL TABLE
OF THE
KINGS OF JUDAH AND ISRAEL,
SHOWING THE PERIOD OF THEIR REIGNS,

JUDAH.	Reigned Years.	B. C	ISRAEL.	Reigned Years
David	40	1070	David	40
Solomon	40	1030	Solomon	40
Rehoboam	17	990	Jeroboam............	22
Abijah	3	973		
Asa	41	970		
		968	Nadab	2
		966	Baasha..............	23
		943	Elah	1
		942	Zimri & Omri........	11
		931	Ahab................	22
Jehoshaphat	25	929		
		909	Ahaziah	2
		907	Jehoram, or Joram ..	12
Jehoram, or Joram ..	8	904		
Ahaziah	1	896		
Athaliah	6	895	Jehu	28
Joash, or Jehoash	40	889		
		887	Jehoahaz............	17
		850	Jehoash, or Joash	16
Amaziah	29	849		
		834	Jeroboam II.	41
Interregnum	11	820		
Uzziah, or Azariah....	52	809		
		793	First Interregnum	22
		771	Zachariah & Shallum .	1
		770	Menahem............	10
		760	Pekahiah	2
		758	Pekah	20
Jotham	16	757		
Ahaz................	16	741		
		738	Second Interregnum ..	10
		728	Hoshea	9
Hezekiah	29	725		
		719	SAMARIA taken	
Manasseh	55	696		
Amon	2	641		
Josiah	31	639		
Jehoahaz & Jehoiakim	11	608		
Jehoiachin & Zedekiah	11	597		
JERUSALEM taken		586		

KINGS OF JUDAH AND ISRAEL.

BEFORE we enter upon the history of the kings of Judah and Israel, it is desirable to consider the nature and character of the record from whence the following brief sketch is to be derived. It has been well observed, that this record is *ancient* history—far more ancient than any other; and while it is complete, authentic, and minute in its details, the most ancient of all other historical records are confessedly fictitious, obscure, or deficient as to material points. This is *true* history, there is no fear of deception; and the few discrepancies which may occasionally appear, will be found confirmatory of the facts, when fully examined. Again, it is *history*, and therefore interesting to every man, as containing records of human life; and instructive, when duly considered, both by way of precept and example. The importance of these considerations is increased beyond calculation, when we bear in mind that it is the history of the Jewish church, the sacred society chosen by the Most High, to keep his blessed word of revelation, and to practise his ordinances—those of prayer and praise, and those of ceremonial import. It is *sacred* history. From the first formation of the Jewish people into a nation, they were placed under a THEOCRACY, a government different from that of every other nation under heaven; inasmuch as God himself entered into covenant with the people, that he would be their KING, and rule among them. This presence was typified by the tabernacle, and afterwards by the temple; which

B

were symbols of his presence, although the Most High dwelleth not in temples made with hands ; and the rulers, whether ecclesiastical or civil, or high priests, judges, or kings, acted as the ministers of Jehovah, acknowledging his presence, and ever consulting ·Him when their hearts were right with their God. And this Theocracy existed under the kings, as well as under Moses, Joshua, and the Judges. Much might be said upon this subject, but it would lead us from the points before us, and it requires distinct consideration and explanation. But, above all, it is not a *mere* history, however superior to all other records in general circumstances ; it is given by inspiration of God, and it is " a part of that blessed book which is to be a standing rule of our faith and practice." Here we listen to the voice of God, and may be assured that not a word has been spoken or recorded without a cause.

The objects brought before our view are numerous and important. Many of the prophecies, and many psalms, are rendered much more clear, by attention to the history connected with them. Several of the characters evidently are typical of Christ ; and many passages, especially those which explain. the prophecies, throw considerable light on the only way of salvation through a crucified Saviour, both God and man, in one Christ. Again, the details are instructive for our guidance as to the concerns of this life. It is true, that the history chiefly embraces details relative to kings and rulers, and should be closely studied by all in supreme authority ; but there are many things which refer directly to the concerns of common life ; and all are instructive, as showing the evil of sin and the beauty of holiness. Even the failings of God's people recorded here may be of use, both to the highest and to the lowest of the children of men. But especially these records are invaluable, as exhibiting God's dealings respecting states and kingdoms ; they declare, as though written with a sunbeam, that "righteousness exalteth a nation, but sin is a reproach to any people." God's providence moves in a mysterious way, and his dealings with men leave much under clouds and darkness, as to his proceedings towards them in this life : yet we know that all shall be made clear in the event ; and we may therefore be contented to leave those matters which appear doubtful to us now.　But this does not apply to nations, states, and kingdoms : we here see them rising or falling, according to their conduct as nations ; and plainly perceive that public bodies, and communities of men, will be punished or rewarded in this world, according to their deeds.　This may indeed be learned from common history, but much more clearly from the sacred records.　Had the common histories of ancient times been equally clear in their early details, how valuable would they have been accounted ; but the early origin of every other nation, besides that of the Jews, is obscured by fabulous accounts and mythological disguise.　Would that the lessons conveyed by holy writ were more constantly kept in view, and more forcibly impressed upon the minds of persons of every rank. The ways of the Lord are still the same ; he has now, as he had of old, a peculiar people amidst the world at large : for these his arm is still exerted, and the course of his providence may be clearly traced by every one who inquires with simplicity and faith—

God of Israel, still the same,
For the glory of thy name,
Let thy people now behold
Mighty works like those of old ;
Works of power, the mountains moving,
Works of grace, thy kindness proving.

DAVID.

REIGNED FORTY YEARS.

[B. C. 1070—1030.*]

By the death of Saul, David was freed from the
dangers which had surrounded him during several
years, and the promise of his elevation to the throne of
Israel appeared likely to be fulfilled without further
delay. But David had learned that the Lord's time
is the best time, and, among other profitable uses' of
adversity, he was taught that his times were in the hands
of the Lord. His first care, therefore, was to obtain
the Divine direction; and in pursuance of this, he proceeded to Hebron with his family and followers, and
there the men of Judah chose him for their king. He
sent an intimation of their choice to the other tribes,
but the jealousy between Ephraim and Judah kept
them from joining their brethren. Abner, the captain
of Saul's army, procured the only surviving son of
Saul to be chosen as king over Israel, intending to govern in his name; as this prince, called Ishbosheth,
was a weak and incapable person. Abner also would
be the less disposed to support David, from having been
personally concerned in Saul's proceedings against him.
David continued in Hebron, unwilling to enter into warfare with his countrymen. It was a strong city, situated
on a hill in the midst of a fertile district, and a spot con-
secrated by the sepulchres of Abraham and other patriarchs. One of David's earliest acts was to send to
the men of Jabesh-gilead, commending their devotedness to Saul; thus showing that he retained no hatred
towards his persecutor, and that attachment to their
late monarch, though his enemy, would not prejudice
him against any Israelites.

* The dates in this work are according to the chronology of *Hales*.

After two years, Abner, and Joab who was the nephew of David, and his principal officer, met near Gibeon, when the former proposed a combat between twelve of their followers on each side, calling it "play:" but such sports are really murder. It ended fatally to all the combatants, and brought on a general engagement, in which the party of Ishbosheth was defeated, but Asahel, the brother of Joab, was slain by Abner; this, although in self-defence, excited the feeling for personal revenge which still is so prevalent in similar cases in the east. The answer of Joab to Abner shows that David's instructions to him were peaceable. Hostilities being thus begun were continued, and to the advantage of David.

After about five years of desultory contests, Ishbosheth quarrelled with Abner, who had taken one of Saul's concubines, a proceeding which indicated an intention to assume royal authority. Abner, offended by his incapable master, negociated with David to bring Israel over to his party. David required the restoration of Michal, his first wife, as a preliminary, probably remembering her affectionate interference to save his life; and Abner, having sent her to him, conferred with the elders of Israel, and afterwards went to David at Hebron. All was settled, but Joab just then returned from an expedition; he was displeased that the king had received the general of Ishbosheth in a friendly manner, blamed David, and recalling Abner by a treacherous message, murdered him under the pretence of an amicable conference, thus risking his master's accession to the national throne to gratify his own private revenge. David was unable to punish his powerful officer, but showed his abhorrence of the murderous treachery by a short but pathetic elegy to Abner's memory, and by persisting to fast, though the people urged him to eat. This is a common method of showing displeasure, still used in the east. We read, that whatsoever the king did pleased all the people: he was well affected towards them, he studied to please them; and, where this is done in a proper and consistent manner, popularity may be obtained without using mean or deceitful arts. The murder of Abner was followed by that of Ishbosheth. The loss of this general had weakened his party, and two of the captains obtaining access to the house of their king, under pretence of drawing the daily supplies of corn for their men—still the usual practice with eastern soldiery—entered his dwelling and went to his private apartments at noon, while he and his attendants were taking the midday repose customary in hot countries. They slew Ishbosheth, and cut off his head, which they carried to David, expecting a reward; but he showed his indignation at their act of blood, by ordering their immediate execution. In his solemn protestation on this occasion, David spoke of the Lord, as Him who had redeemed his soul out of all adversity. The many remarkable preservations in his eventful life had taught him to acknowledge, and to rely upon God alone. The supporters of Saul's family were won over by the forbearance and upright conduct of David, and went to Hebron and made him their king, seven years and a half after the death of Saul. He entered into a solemn league, or covenant, with them before the Lord, doubtless engaging himself to govern according to the Divine law. 2 Sam. v. 2, shows that the Israelites submitted to David, only as to a king appointed by the Lord, and who had shown that he was so by his conduct during the reign of Saul; thus they distinctly recognised the principles of the Theocracy, or Divine Government.

David now was ruler over all Israel; and his first care was to bring the kingdom into order, and one of his early measures for this purpose was to collect the priests and Levites, and to make preparation for due attention to the public ordinances. He found himself surrounded by a powerful host, and moved forward to occupy the strong hold or fortification of Jebus, which being on the northern border of Judah, was a suitable locality for his future residence, and accessible to the other tribes, as well as to his own. This place, from its natural strength, was thought impregnable, and had remained in the hands of the natives ever since the days of Joshua; though, from the head of Goliath being taken there by David, a part at least of the city must have been occupied by the Israelites. The inhabitants ridiculed any attempt to take their city; but David stormed the fort, obtaining entrance through a subterraneous passage, and thus gained possession of the strong hold of Zion. He called it the city of David, and made it his residence, erecting many buildings upon the hill.

The immediate neighbourhood of Jerusalem presents a cluster of barren rocky eminences: as to position, it was well situated both for strength and salubrity: the description of the Psalmist is, "Beautiful for situation, the joy of the whole earth, is Mount Zion, on the sides of the north, the city of the great king." This was the origin of Jerusalem, a city which, for the variety of events connected with it, and especially for those connected with the manifestation of the Son of God in human nature, has been far more remarkable than any other city upon the face of the earth—a city, whose stones and dust forcibly declare the evil and destructive nature of sin. The name Jerusalem signifies "the possession of peace," and it is supposed was first given to the city by David. David removed his family, and settled his government in this place. His family now began to be numerous; he had sons by six wives, having multiplied his alliances, perhaps partly from a desire to strengthen his power. Polygamy then was an allowed practice; but then, as at all times, it destroyed domestic happiness, and excited family discords. A treaty was now entered into between Hiram, king of Tyre, and David. The former appears to have had his regard for the king of Israel founded upon belief in the true God. He "was ever a lover of David," and continued to show the same regard for his son.

During the civil discord between Judah and the other tribes, David remained at Hebron : we do not find that he took part in any battle. He avoided engaging in civil contests : and this accounts for his not making any strong efforts against the son of Saul ; he knew that all would be directed for the best ; but when the Israelites were united, he came forward with his accustomed courage, and the Philistines having renewed hostilities, he defeated them in two hard-fought battles.

On the first invasion of the Philistines, David found it necessary again to occupy the strong hold of Adullam, with which he was so well acquainted, and the Philistines were in the fertile valley of Rephaim, a little to the south of Jerusalem. While preparing to encounter the enemy, David was exhausted by thirst, and recollecting the well of Bethlehem, from whence he had been accustomed to drink in his early days, he expressed an earnest desire for a draught of the water. Three of his most valiant followers, hearing this wish, broke through the army of the Philistines, and brought some of the water to their king. He would not gratify his appetite with the refreshing draught that had been procured at so dear a rate, but poured out the water as an offering to God. A decisive victory was gained, and in the year following the Philistines were again defeated in the same vicinity, when a Divine interference was manifested. A sound betokening the presence of Jehovah was heard, though no visible appearance was seen. David was successful in this war, but the contest was severe ; from 1 Chron. xi. it appears that the Israelites gave way and fled, but some among the chief of those enumerated as " mighty men," withstood the shock of the pursuing enemy, and "the Lord saved them by a great deliverance." The list of David's mighty men contains other incidental notices, probably referring to this period.

David availed himself of the rest from his enemies, to remove the ark from Gibeah to Jerusalem, thus placing the symbolical throne of Jehovah in the royal city, and recognising the Lord as supreme monarch of the nation. A joyful procession was formed for the purpose, and the 68th Psalm was composed for the occasion; but the preparations were made without remembering the injunction, Exodus xxv. 14, that the ark, whenever removed, should be carried on men's shoulders. It was placed on a car, drawn by oxen:

but Uzzah, stretching forth his hand to steady it when shaken by this unlawful method of conveyance, was struck with death ; none but Aaron and his sons were to touch the ark, Numb. iv. 15.   David, alarmed at this event, gave up the idea of removing the ark to Jerusalem at that time, and left it in the house of Obed-edom for three months, during which that family was remarkably blessed.   If the man who had the ark in his house was blessed, how much more so is he that hath the Divine presence in his heart ; and, as *Henry* says, we may have it without fetching it away from our neighbours.

The right preparations being made, the ark was removed with much solemnity, David heading the procession, divested of royal robes, clothed in a priest's garment of linen, and moving with the measured pace usual on occasions of solemn rejoicing.   Sacrifices were offered when the removal began, (it is well for us to seek the Divine blessing at the beginning of an enterprize,) and others were offered when the ark was placed in the tabernacle prepared for it in the city of David. The people were then dismissed to their homes with a liberal present of bread, flesh, and wine.   David's conduct rendered him very popular among his subjects, though he did not act, on this occasion, from a desire to court popularity, but from the right feeling, that all are equal in the sight of God, and should unite in acts of religion.   Michal saw David performing this solemn duty, and showed herself a daughter of Saul; she not only despised him in her heart, but expressed her scorn in opprobrious language, which brought a just rebuke upon her, and may warn us to be careful how we censure actions the reasons for which we cannot understand.   This removal of the ark, it is supposed, also gave occasion for Psalms xxiv. cxxxii. cv. xcvi. and cvi.; and, let us remember, it did not proceed from the mere will of David, but was in compliance with the Divine command; "But unto the place which the Lord your God shall choose out of all your tribes to put his name there, even unto his habitation shall ye seek, and thither thou shalt come : and thither ye shall bring your burnt offerings, and your sacrifices, and your tithes, and heave offerings of your hand, and your vows, and your freewill offerings, and the firstlings of your herds and of your flocks : and there ye shall eat before the Lord your God, and ye shall rejoice in all that ye put your hand unto, ye and your households, wherein the Lord thy God hath blessed thee," Deut. xii. 5—7.

We now pass on to the fifteenth year of David's reign, when his own palace was completed by the

artizans of Tyre. He had formed alliances with the
neighbouring nations, and his greatness had increased
on every side. Still he was mindful of his religious
duties, and desired to honour the ark by erecting a
more permanent building for its reception, and to settle
the principal ordinances of religion at Jerusalem. His
own palace, built and adorned by the most skilful
workmen of that day, must have excited considerable
attention in Palestine, where, as yet, there is reason to
believe, the dwellings were of inferior construction.
The king perceived the superior comforts he enjoyed,
and desired to show his gratitude for these outward
advantages, by honouring the symbol of the Divine
presence.   He was not satisfied to dwell " in a house
of cedar," while the ark of God dwelled " within cur-
tains."   How different the feeling of many wealthy
professors in our day ! They inhabit richly adorned
and sumptuously furnished mansions, while "the houses
of God " in their neighbourhoods are wretched and
inconvenient, and the ministers of the altar are left to
depend upon a scanty pittance, raised with difficulty.
Not so David : having stated his wish to the prophet
Nathan, he was encouraged to proceed ; but that night
a remarkable revelation was made to the prophet.
David was commanded to give up his design, the wars
in which he had been engaged, though in self-defence,
disqualified him for this sacred undertaking.   Surely
this should tend to inspire a horror of bloodshed.   But
a gracious promise was made to David, that the temple he planned should be erected by his son ; also a
promise was given of the future glories of the kingdom
of Christ, who should be his descendant according to
the flesh.   It is plain that David understood that promise as referring to the Messiah. The words, 1 Chron.
xvii. 17, expressly acknowledge this in language of
devout thankfulness ; they may be rendered, " And
thou hast regarded me in the arrangement about the
Man that is to be from above, O God, Jehovah." The
whole of David's devout acknowledgment and humili-

ation on this occasion should be studied, and compared
as it is recorded both in 2 Sam. vii. 18—29, and
1 Chron. xvii. 16—27. He sat before the Lord : he
placed himself in the humble posture in which an inferior places himself at the present day when in the presence of an eastern superior, partly sitting and partly
kneeling, that is, resting his body on his heels.   The
following Psalms appear to be connected with the precious promise given at this time, Psalms ii. xlv. xxii.
xvi. cxviii. cx. These Psalms, it will be found, distinctly
notice the authority and Divinity of Christ, his sufferings and crucifixion, his death and resurrection, his
rejection by the Jews and the reception of the gospel
by the Gentiles, and the exaltation, kingdom and priesthood of the Messiah. By this solemnity, and by these
instructive and animating psalms, David appears to
have made a deep impression on the minds of the
people, establishing them in the worship of Jehovah,
without recourse to severe measures against idolatry.
David was, in many respects, a precursor and type of
the Prince of Peace, the Gospel King, before whom
every enemy shall bow.

> Thus the eternal Father spake
> To Christ the Son ; " Ascend and sit
> At my right hand, till I shall make
> Thy foes submissive at thy feet.
>
> " From Zion shall thy word proceed,
> Thy word, the sceptre in thy hand,
> Shall make the hearts of rebels bleed,
> And bow their wills to thy command.
>
> " That day shall show thy power is great,
> When saints shall flock with willing minds,
> And sinners crowd thy temple-gate,
> Where holiness in beauty shines."

David was again called to active warfare. He subdued the Philistines, took from them Gath, and formed
a life-guard from the people of these districts, which
adhered faithfully to him. He also conquered the
Moabites and the Syrians, extending his dominions to
the Euphrates. Turning from the north towards the

south, he defeated the Edomites, and placed garrisons in their country.   This was an important conquest, as it opened the navigation of the Red Sea, and the trade with the countries to the east, for his successors.   The intercourse between David and Hiram the king of Tyre, perhaps led to the occupation of this district, affording so important a position for commerce with the east.   In this warfare David took an active personal part, but his life was preserved, his fame was spread abroad, and the surrounding nations submitted to him.

In about eighteen years David was enabled to finish successfully eight wars.   1. The civil war with Ish-bosheth.   2. Against the Jebusites.   3. Against the Philistines and their allies.   4. Against the Philistines alone.   5. Against the Moabites.   6. Against Hada-dezer.   7. Against Edom.   8. Against the Ammonites and Syrians.   None of these were undertaken with a desire for conquest or aggrandizement.   The rapid pro-gress of the kingdom of David is a remarkable instance of the Divine power, when we consider the very low state of Israel at the death of Saul, and the civil con-tests which followed and farther weakened the land.

In 1 Chron. xxvii. 25—34, is an account of the ar-rangements made by David for the collection of his revenue ; also the names of his chief officers.   In those days the royal revenues were chiefly collected in arti-cles of produce, and a portion of the land was culti-vated for the support of the monarch's establishment ; we find mention of numerous storehouses, of superin-tendents of tillers of the soil, vineyards, and olive plantations, flocks and herds.   The preceding verses contain an account of the military establishment, which was regulated so that 24,000 men were upon duty every month in rotation, and thus David was always prepared against an enemy, without having recourse to a disorderly general levy of the people, upon the pres-sure of the moment, when danger was at hand.   Nor should the alliance of David with Hiram king of

c

Tyre, be forgotten; it was a measure which strengthened both states against their adversaries.

David was again at leisure, and the first action recorded of this period is pleasing. He sought out the
survivors of the house of Saul to show kindness to
them ; and finding that Mephibosheth, the son of Jonathan, was still alive, he made an ample and honourable provision for his support, by restoring to him the
paternal estate of Saul, and also arranging for his residence at court. But the next circumstance mentioned
was introductory to a most painful event. In the eighteenth year of his reign, David sent ambassadors to
congratulate and condole with the young king of Ammon. He had newly succeeded to that throne, on the
death of his father, who had showed kindness to David
during the persecutions of Saul. The young prince, by
the bad advice of his counsellors, insulted these ambassadors in a manner which would still be considered
grossly affronting to any one in the east. He caused
their beards to be shaved, and the long skirts of their
garments to be cut away. Two similar instances of
insulting ambassadors, by shaving off their beards, are
recorded in the modern history of Persia. This insult
led to a war, in which at first the Syrians took part ;
but they were defeated, and made peace with Israel,
and left the Ammonites without help. David committed the conduct of the war to Joab, and remained
at Jerusalem, indulging in ease and indolence.

The way of sin is a down-hill road, and one evil step
leads on to another with increasing rapidity. What began with indolence, ended in adultery and murder! David seduced Bathsheba, the wife of Uriah, one of Joab's
officers ; and finding that he could not cloak his sin,
he caused the husband to be murdered. Joab readily
executed the wicked command, and immediately afterwards the king married her whom he had thus made a
widow. Among the invaluable peculiarities of Scripture history, we here notice a very important one—

that a plain simple statement of facts is always given,
without any attempt to excuse sin or extenuate guilt;
and this is no where more fully shown than with regard
to the aggravated guilt into which David plunged.
The facts are distinctly related, and the painful consequences are plainly recounted. No censures can be
expressed stronger than those of the guilty transgressor
himself in the 51st Psalm, when awakened to a sense
of his sin.   But let not any one misrepresent David's
crimes, by speaking of them as the fruits or results of
the doctrines of faith ; they are the effects of corrupt
nature ; and since every believer experiences with St.
Paul, that the seeds of evil are in his heart, let every
one earnestly pray that his senses, imaginations, and
desires, may be closed against all forbidden objects.
If we examine this painful history in all its bearings,
we shall be satisfied that no one will be tempted to
make light of David's fall, unless desirous of an excuse
for sin.   David attempted none for himself, and many,
it may be fully believed, have been warned against sin
by his fall, rendered more watchful as to their conduct, and more fervent in prayer, and thus have been
kept from sinning.   Let us be fully satisfied that this
awful guilt never would have been recorded, but for
the good of mankind at large, clearly to show the danger of temptation, and the evil of sin.

For a short time David remained insensible to the
heinousness of his guilt.   It is thought, that during this
interval the Ammonites were conquered, and treated
with cruel harshness by David ; whether his proceedings were such, or whether he only condemned them to
bondage, is not certain ; but David, when dead in sin,
could not have communed with his God as in former
times ; and while the heart is closed against Divine intercourse, and when a lively sense of Divine mercy is
lost, the heart is less disposed to exercise compassion
towards others.

Nathan was sent to reprove David ; and awakened

him to a sense of his sin, by recounting an affecting tale
of oppression, and then showing how applicable it was
to his own case. His words, " Thou art the man," were

sent home directly to the conscience of the monarch ; he
attempted not to evade the application, but at once fully
confessed his guilt, and sought for pardon. The pardon
thus sought was not denied ; but as this deed had given
occasion to the enemies of the Lord to blaspheme, severe punishments were denounced, to last through the
remainder of his reign. David expressed his deep
sorrow in the 51st Psalm, where it will be seen, as
already remarked, that he sought not to excuse or to
make light of his awful guilt, while he earnestly prayed
for that renewal of the heart, and those influences of
the Holy Spirit, which alone could secure him for the
future : and this deeply affecting composition may be
used to express the state and the feelings of every
truly repenting sinner, who is aware of the extent of
the evil of his heart—

Lord, I am vile, conceiv'd in sin ;
And born unholy and unclean :
Sprung from the man whose guilty fall
Corrupts the race, and taints us all.

Behold I fall before thy face,
My only refuge is thy grace ;
No outward forms can make me clean ;
The leprosy lies deep within.

While guilt disturbs and breaks my peace,
Nor flesh nor soul hath rest or ease ;
Lord, let me hear the pardoning voice,
And bid my mournful heart rejoice.

Other Psalms are considered as having reference to
this painful and affecting history, as Psalm vi. xxxii.
xxxviii. xxxix. xl. xli. and ciii.; the last is a psalm
of thanksgiving for mercies, and what mercy is equal
to a sense of the pardon of sin ? Some indeed consider that one or more of these psalms refer to a severe
affliction by sickness, by which David suffered about
this time, and, if that were the case, it might be connected with his mental sufferings, for the mind and the
body often act upon and influence each other.

We now must proceed to the events which crowded
rapidly upon each other during the remainder of
David's life. The splendour and prosperity which
marked the commencement and middle of his reign
departed, and a gloomy and disastrous period followed.
Crimes of the blackest die were committed by his
children ; he was driven from his throne for a time by
the rebellion of his favourite son ; we see him forsaken
by the friends he had most trusted, the affections of his
subjects alienated, and never fully regained, and the
strength of his kingdom weakened by these dissensions,
and by a pestilence, brought upon his subjects by his
own unadvised proceeding. At length he died, broken
in constitution beyond what might have been expected
at his years. See David in his latter days ; contrast
his state with that of former times, when he stood
strong in the Divine favour, and then say whether the
consequences of his sin were not bitter indeed, and

such as, beyond comparison, to outweigh the momentary gratification of any lust : but how much more dreadful the result, had David been allowed to go on in carnal security, or to die impenitent!

David had a pledge of forgiveness in the birth of Solomon, with the gracious assurance sent by the prophet Nathan, that the child should enjoy the Divine favour ; and he soon needed such support, for troubles speedily began to cloud his sky. The first was an outrage committed by his eldest son Amnon, towards his sister Tamar. David was wroth, but punished not his son as he deserved. As a parent, he was too indulgent, and probably the sense of his own bad example might restrain the hand of justice on this occasion. Let parents think how fatal may be the results of their bad examples to their children. How bitter the pang to hear a child say, either in this world or the next, " Father," (or mother,) " to *you* I owe my untimely end ; you did not correct me, nor warn me of the fatal consequences of a sinful course!" but how much more bitter, when the parent has been the agent of Satan, setting a bad example, or even being the direct instrument to lead the child into the ways of perdition ; and such parents there are!

About two years after, in the twenty-fifth of David's reign, Absalom avenged his sister's wrong, by the premeditated murder of his brother Amnon, in the presence of their brethren, at the festivity of a sheep-shearing. This still deeper act of guilt could not be expected to remain unpunished. Absalom therefore fled to his grandfather, the king of Geshur, and remained with him three years, when Joab employed a woman to bring a supposititious case of family troubles for the king's decision, and by a politic intercession, working upon the parental weakness of David, obtained pardon for Absalom, and permission for him to return. But two years more passed before he was admitted into his father's presence. During that interval he was confined to his own house, a restraint which this insolent youth could ill brook ;

he compelled Joab again to intercede for him, who
again did so with success ; but the undue partiality of
the father brought its own punishment.

The vain and ambitious young man studied the arts
of popularity, accusing his father of want of attention
to his subjects. If David was afflicted with heavy
sickness at any part of his reign, probably it was now,
and that might furnish some grounds for the artful mis-
representation, that he neglected to administer justice.
But Absalom proceeded to form a conspiracy, which
four years after, in the thirty-fourth year of David's
kingly power, broke out into open rebellion. At Hebron, where David spent the first years of his reign,
the standard of revolt was raised. Proclamation was
made, " Absalom reigneth in Hebron." Many were
induced to join the rebellion from various motives,
and not a few were led to countenance the assemblage
without knowledge of any evil design, and thus were
drawn in to unite with the party of Absalom, though
had the proposal been openly made, they would have
rejected it. Is not this a warning to every one to be
careful how he allows himself to join in public measures,
without having fully weighed the possible results?
There had been enough in the conduct of Absalom, to
put any true friend of his father on his guard against
giving countenance to the son, though only at a sacrifice and a feast. But others came, well knowing that
such a rebellion was planned ; and it is observable that
Ahithophel, the wisest counsellor of David, was forward
in the conspiracy. There appears reason to suppose
that he was the grandfather of Bathsheba, and some
consider that what had passed relative to her, might
have been the principal cause for his engaging against
his king, and perhaps even planning this rebellion.

David was alarmed at the news of this revolt, and
of the numbers openly opposed to him so close at
hand ; he was overcome by the painful fact, that the
hearts of the men of Israel were with Absalom. He
again showed reluctance to shed the blood of his

subjects, and immediately left Jerusalem, with his family and servants, and many other adherents, most of 'whom he sent on before-hand towards Jordan, not seeking to protect himself by placing his friends in danger.   As he was unwilling to involve others unnecessarily in his troubles, David advised Ittai, the leader of the Gittites, to return with his men to the city ; but this faithful body-guard determined to adhere to their benefactor.   Zadok and Abiathar, with the priests and Levites, came forth to accompany David, bearing the ark.   But he, with a right feeling, resolved to leave the matter to God, and refused to allow the ark to be carried from Jerusalem, well aware that the Divine presence was not restricted to the outward symbol, and not desiring to appear to rest his own and his people's success thereon, an error which had been so fatal to the sons of Eli.   He also directed the priests to return, that they might send him word what passed in the city.   He then crossed the brook Kedron, and took the road towards Jericho, passing over Mount Olivet ; and went up the ascent barefoot, weeping and with his head covered, which are eastern marks of humiliation and sorrow.   How painful the feelings which must have passed through his mind when he looked back upon the city he had built, and adorned, and where he had spent so many years of glory and happiness ! But his chief regret was his being compelled to leave the place where he enjoyed the Divine presence in the public ordinances, where he sat before the ark, and went with the multitude to the house of God.

David was told that Ahithophel, his wisest counsellor and intimate friend, had joined Absalom, but this also he left with God, praying that the counsel of Ahithophel might be turned into foolishness. He then met a faithful aged counsellor, Hushai, who was prepared to accompany him in his flight, but David sent him back to counteract the crafty advice of the traitor, if opportunity presented. Other circumstances are related. Ziba, the servant of Mephibosheth, by a present and a false report of the desertion of the son of Saul, obtained a grant of his master's land. A little further ón, David was insulted and cursed by Shimei, a relative of Saul, but he refused to let Abishai punish him, leaving this trouble also with the Lord, and submitting with resignation to the insult.

Absalom entered Jerusalem immediately after his father had left the city. Ahithophel then directed the rebellious youth to proceedings which showed the deepest enmity towards his father: Also he urged an immediate pursuit, which would have ensured his destruction ; but the Lord turned the counsel of Ahithophel into foolishness, and Absalom, at the suggestion of Hushai, resolved to delay sending a chosen band to pursue his father. On this the treacherous counsellor, Ahithophel, despaired of the ultimate success of the revolt, and his pride was offended at the rejection of his advice. He went home and hanged himself; thus becoming his own executioner, and affording an example of the retributive providence of God.

David and his followers halted in the wilderness, where the priests conveyed to him an account of Ahithophel's advice. By a forced night march the fugitives reached Jordan ; they crossed the river before morning, and halted not till they arrived at Mahanaim, in the farthest part of the tribe of Gad, where they were received with hospitality and kindness. The circumstances recorded in the whole description are very similar to what would take place on a like occasion in the east at the present day, when the same articles would be provided for a destitute and fugitive prince and his companions. Absalom followed with the mass of the people who had joined him ; they outnumbered the supporters of David, although he was aided by others in that district. A battle was inevitable, but the followers of David would not allow the monarch to risk his life in the combat, when, still too regardless of the crime of his unnatural son, he charged the leaders to deal gently with the young man Absalom !

The battle was fought in the wood of Ephraim, a country not suited for the encounter of armies, being partly a morass, and partly overgrown with wood, full of precipices, and pits, and swamps, so that many lost their lives among them, some fugitives possibly were destroyed by wild beasts which harboured in the thickets. The followers of Absalom were defeated with a great slaughter, and he himself, riding fast to escape the servants of David, was caught by his head in the

boughs of an oak, and the mule on which he rode passed away and left him suspended among the branches. Being entangled by his hair, which is elsewhere said to have been particularly long and beautiful, and which he was accustomed to cherish with great care, he could not extricate himself. It is not uncommon for sufferings to proceed from objects of which we have been particularly vain. Yes, many a sufferer cut off in the prime of life, " could tell what ills from beauty spring," or lament the time and abilities mispent in useless attentions to the perishing body.

Joab being told where Absalom was entangled, immediately hastened to the place, and with the prompt and stern decision which marked his character, disregarding David's orders for mercy, slew this rebellious son, knowing that the revolt depended upon Absalom's life ; he then recalled the followers of David from the pursuit of their brethren. Thus Absalom died, the victim of his own rebellious attempt against his father. He had, when living, caused a splendid sepulchre to be hewn out for himself, in a rock near Jerusalem, but his burial-place was a pit in the wood of Ephraim, and his monument a heap of stones thrown upon his body ; precisely the end commanded by the law for a rebellious son ! Let every youthful reader contemplate him with abhorrence.

> ———— We turn us from thy tomb,
> Usurping prince ! Thy beauty and thy grace
> Have perish'd with thee, but thy fame survives—
> The ingrate son, that pierc'd a father's heart !

David sat in the gate, an apartment of the tower at the entrance to the city of Mahanaim, whence there was an extended view of the country. He sat watching for intelligence of the event of the combat, and when informed that his adherents were victorious, his only inquiry was, " Is the young man Absalom safe ? " Such was his foolish fondness for a wicked son ; and on learning the death of Absalom from a second messenger, who expressed himself in that guarded phraseology which would be used in the east at the present day, the parent broke out into an excessive display of grief, which nothing could justify under his circumstances, though it may be partly excused by the feelings which as a parent he must have had for a son dying in such an awful state of open sin and impenitence. The indulgence of this grief threatened to retard the restoration of David's power ; but Joab rebuked the king with much warmth, and, roused from his improper display of sorrow, he appeared in public to receive the congratulations of the people.

A minute account is given of David's return to Jerusalem. As usual, many who had stood aloof from
assisting the fugitive king, or who had even acted
against him, now hastened to welcome his return ; and
the people who had followed Absalom appeared more
ready than the adherents of David. This may have
partly arisen from the king's displeasure against his
faithful though disrespectful supporters, the sons of his
sister Zeruiah. Joab and Abishai had always shown
the most unshaken loyalty towards their uncle, but
they did not treat him with that deferential respect to
which, as an absolute eastern prince, David had now
become accustomed. The firm conduct of Joab, in
putting Absalom to death, brought these feelings of
jealousy to a greater height ; and instead of showing
regard to his faithful supporter, who so effectually
served him in the recent difficulty, David dismissed
Joab from the honourable office of captain of the host,
and appointed Amasa, another of his nephews, who
had been the chief commander under Absalom, to be
the successor !

This very doubtful appointment did not long continue. A dispute, connected with the king's return to
Jerusalem, arose between the people of Judah and
those of the other tribes. Sheba, a man of influence,
of the tribe of Benjamin, drew away the people of
Israel, and seems to have had some intention to usurp
the kingly power. Amasa was sent to assemble the
men of Judah, and to crush this new revolt ; but failing to do so by the appointed day, Abishai was ordered by David to take the armed bands that formed
his life-guard, and pursue Sheba. Joab went forth as
a volunteer, and when Amasa joined them, and would
have taken the command, Joab hesitated not to as-
sassinate him in the same treacherous manner he had
manifested towards Abner. Joab then pursued Sheba,
who took refuge in a remote town in the northern part
of the land, and proceeded to besiege the place ; but
a wise female, apprehensive that her people would be

made sufferers from a dispute in which they had taken no part, suggested to Joab to propose terms of peace. He agreed to be satisfied if Sheba was given up; the inhabitants put the rebel to death, and threw his head over the wall to Joab, who returned to Jerusalem with the head of Sheba, a proof of his victory, and retained his former office and power, till the death of David, notwithstanding the displeasure of the king. The proceeding of this " wise woman" ought not to pass without our notice ; it shows the wisdom of seeking peace by requiring and offering explanation ; and the christian who feels that an enemy is within, desirous to lead him into rebellion, may learn from hence to listen to the requirements of his rightful sovereign : let the traitor be expelled or cut off, let him " ask counsel at Abel, and so end the matter." It should especially be impressed upon the youthful reader, to bear in mind, that a few calm words of inquiry, and the manifestation of a desire for peace, will often save himself, and others also, from very serious evils.

Several of the Psalms were written during this rebellion. Psalms iii. vii. xlii. xliii. lv. iv. v. lxii. cxliii. cxliv. lxx. and lxxi. are attributed to this period. They show the humbled spirit of David, that he acknowledged the justice of his punishment and threw himself wholly upon the Lord's mercy. We also see, that he cast his burden upon the Lord, looking to God to sustain him, and it was no light burden which then pressed him down. To see a beloved son, and a valued counsellor, actually aiming at his life, was a great trial to the father and the king.

> Were it my foe my ruin sought,
>   I might have borne his rage and spite;—
> But 'tis my partner; 'tis my guide,
>   My prov'd companion and my friend,
> With whom sweet counsel I have tried,
>   And lov'd God's temple to attend.

Three years' famine succeeded the rebellion; it was sent as a national punishment, on account of the massacre of the Gibeonites by Saul and his bloody house.

D

When this event took place is not recorded, but it
evidently was an act of violence of that wicked monarch, in opposition to the Divine direction that they
should be spared.   Some have considered that Saul
provided for his family and kindred by the massacre
of the Gibeonites, and the confiscation of their pos-
sessions, to the grant of which he may refer, 1 Sam.
xxii. 7.   These cities of the Gibeonites were in the
lot of the tribe of Benjamin, and it is possible that
the persons who now suffered, had been guilty parties
in this act of spoliation.   The deeds of the bloody
house, or murderous family of Saul, are expressly
stated as having led to this judicial proceeding, and,
with one exception, those men were the only survivors
of that guilty house.   We must, however, be contented
to leave this matter in obscurity, among other mysteries
in God's providential dealings, assured that all is right,
and will be found to be so in the end.   The nation
at large deserved punishment for their late rebellion,
and the family of Saul appears to have taken an active
part therein.   Two sons of Saul, by his concubine
Rizpah, and five grandsons by his eldest daughter
Merab, were executed by the Gibeonites ; and the
whole of that family was now cut off, excepting the
son of Jonathan, whom David spared ; and as he was
the lineal successor of Saul, it was plain that David
did not destroy the family from any feelings of apprehension with regard to the succession to the throne.   ·

The Philistines, probably, were encouraged by the
weakened state of the land, from rebellion and famine,
as we find that they again took up arms, about the
thirty-seventh year of the reign of David.   After four
battles, they were finally conquered, and the gigantic
kindred of Goliath were slain.   David had nearly lost
his life in the first battle, but was rescued by Abishai,
and the people would not consent to his going out
again to battle.   After these wars, David appears to
have been directed to make a revision of Psalm xviii.
and thus left it in the form in which it is in 2 Samuel

xxii. This sublime poem is a summary of the signal
mercies David had experienced; he attributes all his
victories and deliverances to his God.

About two years before the death of David, he was
tempted into another offence against the Lord. In
the pride of his heart, he resolved to number his subjects. For this there was no necessity at the time,
and the measure was commanded in a spirit of vanity
and presumption, and with circumstances which even
Joab considered reprehensible. It is probable that
some design or desire of foreign conquest was entertained; and ascertaining the number of disposable
warriors would be the first step to a course directly
contrary to the Divine precepts respecting the Hebrew
nation, which forbad their attempting foreign conquest,
or warfare, beyond the boundaries of the promised land.
The total number able to bear arms was 1,300,000,
evidently a vast increase from the population of the
nation at the death of Saul, only forty years before.
Nor was the enumeration quite completed, the people
of Benjamin, and the Levites, were not counted.
Some indications of Divine wrath hindered Joab from
finishing the work, and David himself, after more than
nine months insensibility, was convinced that he had
done wrong, this was confirmed by a message from
the Lord, telling him to choose as a national punishment, either three years of famine, three months of
defeat, or three days of pestilence. David chose the
latter, as more directly evidencing the hand of God.

The destroying angel went forth, and 70,000 fell as
victims. The destruction was coming upon Jerusalem,
when a glimpse of the Divine appearance was permitted to David and his elders, who were clothed in
sackcloth, and in the posture of humiliation. The
repenting king prayed that he might be punished instead of his people. His humiliation was accepted,
and he was commanded to build an altar, and to offer
sacrifices on Mount Moriah, over which the angel
visibly appeared to David and to others. The king

refused to accept as a gift the threshing floor which
then occupied the upper part of this eminence, and
purchased it at its full value, from Ornan, the owner,

a descendant from the ancient Jebusites. He then
offered sacrifices, which were consumed by fire from
heaven, as an evidence that they were accepted, and
that the Lord had now chosen the mount as the place
for his special worship ; this caused David to select it,
as the site for the building erected in the place of the
tabernacle. The place is still pointed out by tokens
which cannot be mistaken; and it is not subject to
the same legendary mistakes as other places in Jerusalem. A mohammedan mosque now stands where
the temple once shone radiant in the noontide sun ;
it marks the place where Ornan drove his oxen over
the corn, where David and his elders saw the angel
revealed to their view, and probably it marks also the
place where Abraham stood ready to sacrifice his
beloved Isaac, in obedience to the Divine command,
when his hand was stayed.

Only a few months now remained to David upon earth, but they were embittered by the conduct of another child. Feeble and wasted, his grey hairs brought down with sorrow to the borders of the grave, Adonijah would not even wait for the natural course of events, but sought to wrest the sceptre from his dying father's hand. He followed the plans of Absalom, and sought popularity; he succeeded in drawing over Joab and Abiathar to his party, and was supported by his brethren; excepting Solomon, who was intended by their father for his successor, and had been designated as such by Divine appointment. David, feeble and unable to make any personal effort, sent those attendants who remained faithful, to proclaim Solomon without delay, and anoint him king. The conspirators, engaged in a public entertainment given by Adonijah, during which they saluted him as their monarch, were struck with fear at the prompt and decisive course adopted, and hastened to their own houses without offering any direct opposition to the new monarch. Adonijah took refuge at the altar, and was pardoned upon condition of future good conduct.

The appointment of Solomon to the throne was confirmed in a public assembly, called by the king. On this occasion David related his desire to build a house of rest for the ark of the covenant, in which the Lord's presence might be manifested, but which work, as we have seen, the Lord had forbidden him to pursue. He publicly stated that the reason was, that he had been engaged in war, and had shed blood. None of David's wars were contests of aggression or conquest, and though valiant in battle, he had nothing of the spirit of a worldly warrior about him; yet this work was not to be carried forward by him who had been engaged in warfare, but by a son who was expressly to be a man of peace. David proceeded to address Solomon in the beautiful words set forth 1 Chron. xxviii. 9, 10, " And thou, Solomon my son, know thou the God of thy father, and serve him with a perfect heart

and with a willing mind : for the Lord searcheth all
hearts, and understandeth all the imaginations of the
thoughts : if thou seek him, he will be found of thee ;
but if thou forsake him, he will cast thee off for ever.
Take heed now ; for the Lord hath chosen thee to build
an house for the sanctuary : be strong, and do it."

After this, David gave Solomon directions, explain-
ing the plan of the house, and the buildings by which
it was to be surrounded ; he made over to him the vast
treasures he had amassed for the building, with its
various articles of furniture and utensils. A part of
these treasures had been collected even by Saul and
Samuel, and Abner and Joab, and was dedicated by
them to the service of the Lord, 1 Chron. xxvi. 28.
The king also called upon the princes to contribute, and
they offered willingly, with perfect heart. David notices
this readiness in the beautiful thanksgiving, 1 Chron.
xxix. 10—19, wherein. he acknowledges that all the
store prepared for the Lord's house is God's own, and
came of his hand.

The congregation joined in blessing the Lord, and
in offering sacrifices ; thus Solomon was publicly and
with solemnity made king, also Zadok was appointed
high priest in the place of Abiathar. The 72nd
Psalm may be regarded as being connected with this
period of David's history ; it is a psalm for Solomon,
and contains a prophetic view of the peaceful glories
of his reign. But we soon perceive that " a greater
than Solomon is here ;" passages of larger and deeper
import crowd upon us : evidently the glories of the
Messiah and his kingdom were present to the mind of
the inspired writer. Of Him alone can it be said,

> With power he vindicates the just,
> And treads tho' oppressor in the dust ;
> His worship and his fear shall last
> Till hours, and years, and time be past.

The preparations made for the temple, included
gold, silver, precious stones, brass, iron, with other requisite materials, to a very large amount. The precise

value cannot be ascertained, while considerable difference of opinion exists as to the sum, but at the lowest
computation· it was equal to several millions of pounds
of English money.   David's power had been very
great for several years, and he had collected the spoil
of the vanquished nations with a design for this appro-
priation ; among these the idols would contribute
largely, Psa. cxv. 4 ; cxxxv. 15.   From the mention of
the gold of Ophir, 1 Chron. xxix. 4, it would appear ↴
that David began that traffic with the east, from
whence Solomon afterwards derived a vast influx of
wealth.   The access to the Red Sea, obtained by the
conquest of Edom, might induce David to attempt this
commerce. ˙ His subjects also very readily dedicated
the articles of wealth which they possessed.   We
may easily imagine that the property of a similar description in our own country would amount to a vast
sum, if offered with equal willingness ; among a pastoral people of simple manners, like those of Israel at
that day, there would not exist the same fancied motives for refusing to dedicate their valuables to the service of the Lord, which actuate their possessors, in the
coldness and indifference of modern times.

Connected with˙ the latter days of David, were the
appointments recorded 1 Chron. xxiii. to xxvi.   They
show the regularity which David introduced into the
Divine services before the erecting the temple, and
in preparation for it. From some passages, (see 1 Chron.
ix. 18 ; xxvi. 28 ;) it appears that the design of regulat-
ing these services, as well as that of erecting the
temple, had been formed even in the days of Samuel.
We may, without difficulty, suppose that David and
the prophet conferred on the subject, and that Samuel
gave directions and advice to his youthful friend, doubtless under Divine inspiration.   The instructions were
very minute ; David also expressly stated that he had
received the Divine direction.   It is important to notice how he supported the authority requisite for the
tribe of Levi, yet did not give up the government to

them, nor hesitate to prescribe compliance with such
rules and arrangements as appeared needful.

The final directions given by David to Solomon
have been misunderstood and misrepresented. He did
not direct that Joab and Shimei should be put to
death ; but as they had proved themselves to be very
ungovernable and dangerous characters, Solomon was
instructed to keep a close watch upon them, in order
to punish any future treasonable conduct as soon as it
was manifested, without allowing it to go on to any
extent. The last words of the dying monarch are recorded 2 Sam. xxiii. 1—7.

Thus expired the Divinely-appointed king, the
sweet psalmist of Israel : in the latter character, especially, he claims the attention of every christian. It
has been well observed, that " The songs which
charmed the solitude of the desert caves of Engedi, or
resounded from the voice of the Hebrew people as
they wound along the glens and hill-sides of Judea,
have been repeated for ages in almost every part of
the habitable world ; in the remotest islands of the
ocean, among the forests of America, and the sands of
Africa. How many human hearts have they softened,
purified, exalted ! of how many wretched beings have
they been the secret consolation ! on how many communities have they drawn down the blessings of Divine Providence, by bringing the affections into unison
with their deep devotional fervour." This statement
is correct, but it goes not far enough ; the philosophical
divine may not be inclined or able to point out the
key-note, which touches alike the heart of the monarch
and the cottager, if devoted followers of Christ : it is
this, " Every psalm either points to Christ, or may be
so applied as to lead the believer's thoughts to Him.
The Psalms are the language of the believer's heart,
under its various exercises, whether mourning for sin,
thirsting after God, or rejoicing in Him ; whether bur-
dened with affliction, struggling with temptation, or
triumphing in the hope or enjoyment of deliverance ;

whether admiring the Divine perfections, thanking
God for his mercies, meditating on his truths, or de-
lighting in his service, they form a Divinely-appointed
standard of genuine experience, by which we may
judge ourselves.   Their value in this view is inestimable ; and the use of them will generally increase with
the growth of true religion in the heart.   If we make
the Psalms familiar to us, as we ought to do, whatever errand we have at the throne of grace, by way
of confession, petition, or thanksgiving, we may be
assisted from thence ; whatever devout affection is
working in us, whatever holy desire or hope, sorrow
or joy, we may there find words to clothe it—sound
speech which cannot be condemned.   In the language
of this Divine book, the prayers and praises of the
church have been offered up to the throne of grace
from age to age."   How superior this latter view of
this blessed book to the cold though beautiful expressions first quoted! flowers may catch the eye and be
pleasing objects to the outward senses, but they impart
no nourishment or strength ; for such advantages we
must seek the fruit, and, blessed be God, the result of
the study of Scripture is abundantly exhibited in the
experience of believers of every age.   We shall find
that it is important to read the testimonies and records
of such men in christian biographies, as, although uninspired, they show the happiness which results from
attention to the word of God.

The last words of David, already quoted, demand
attention.   Whether they were spoken by him when
actually upon his death-bed, or when declining strength
gave indication of the approach of his last hour, is not
material ; but it is important to observe, that they in-
clude a prophecy of the Messiah in his Divine glory
and his righteous reign.   David considers his own
undeserved exaltation, he refers to the duty of rulers,
and could not but regret that his house was not with
God as it should have been ; but he was permitted to
trust in the everlasting covenant, ordered in all things

and sure.   He felt the evil and burden of sin, and lamented the weakness of his faith, fear, and love, and
looked forward to the glories of Christ's kingdom on
earth, and his own enjoyment of a better rest.

> Thus hath the Son of Jesse said,
> When Israel's God had rais'd his head
>   To high imperial sway:
> Struck with his last poetic fire,
> Zion's sweet Psalmist tun'd his lyre
>   To this harmonious lay.
>
> " Thus dictates Israel's sacred Rock:
> Thus hath the God of Jacob spoke
>   By my responsive tongue:
> Behold the Just One over men
> Commencing his religious reign,
>   Great subject of my song!
>
> So gently shines with genial ray
> The' unclouded lamp of rising day,
>   And cheers the tender flowers,
> When midnight's soft diffusive rain
> Hath bless'd the gardens and the plain
>   With kind refreshing showers.
>
> Shall not my house this honour boast ?
> My soul the' eternal cov'nant trust,
>   Well-order'd still and sure ?
> There all my hopes and wishes meet :
> In death I call its blessings sweet,
>   And feel its bond secure.
>
> The sons of Belial shall not spring,
> Who spurn at heav'n's appointed King,
>   And scorn his high command :
> Tho' wide the briars infest the ground,
> And the sharp-pointed thorns around
>   Defy a tender hand ;
>
> A dreadful warrior shall appear
> With iron arms, and massy spear,
>   And tear them from their place :
> Touch'd with the lightning of his ire,
> At once they kindle into fire,
>   And vanish in the blaze."

If the personal character and conduct of David is
considered, he must be pronounced superior to any
hero of Gentile antiquity, and no other of the Hebrew
kings can be compared with him. Let the traits of his
character be examined, and due admiration given to

his youthful piety, his undaunted courage, his noble spirit, his varied abilities, his kindness and his affection in his domestic relations, his justice as a ruler, and his support of his lawful superior, though his enemy ; but, above all, we have to admire his constant, unvarying adherence to the worship of Jehovah. His latter days, we have seen, were troubled, which shows the Divine justice in the punishment of sin ; this was not passed by in David any more than in Saul. In no other instance, recorded either in common or in sacred history, do we more clearly see that virtue was rewarded and vice punished, than in the case of David. He was "a man after God's own heart," such a one as fulfilled the Divine purposes, design, and intention *willingly :* he did not, like Saul, set himself in opposition thereto ; but he faithfully performed the pleasure of God, by willingly devoting himself to the furtherance of the great events he was raised up to accomplish. Whatever may be the views of philosophic historians, it is certain that a more truly illustrious personage than David, cannot be pointed out in the records of the world.

> Thus David slept, the great, the wise, the go d ;
> The man who long by Heaven's appointment, stood
> His country's friend ; who met the giant foe,
> While yet a ruddy youth, and laid him low ;
> The patriot prince, who guided Israel's bands
> With firm "integrity, and skilful hands;"
> The holy seer, who, rapt to future times,
> Sang of Messiah, dying for the crimes
> Of countless ages—his illustrious Son,
> His glorious deeds, his reign on earth begun ;
> The sacred hand, who oft attuned the lyre
> To themes prophetic, with a prophet's fire ;
> He who with Israel's God communed, and wept
> O'er Israel's wrongs, and Israel's honour kept,
> A trust inviolate, from men of blood—
> Great David softly slept—he sl pt in God,
> "Of honour, days, and riches full—a calm release,
> And to his fathers laid," reposed in peace.

See page 29.

SOLOMON.

REIGNED FORTY YEARS.

[B. C. 1030—990.]

SOLOMON was the son of David and Bathsheba, born after his repentance and the forgiveness of his sin. The expectation of David concerning this son was raised by the prediction, recorded 1 Chron. xxii. 9, 10 ; " Behold, a son shall be born to thee, who shall be a man of rest ; and I will give him rest from all his enemies round about : for his name shall be So- lomon, and I will give peace and quietness unto Israel in his days. He shall build a house for my name ; and he shall be my son, and I will be his father ; and I

will establish the throne of his kingdom over Israel for
ever." Though this declaration had a reference to the
son and successor of David, yet it was only verified
fully in the Messiah, the Prince of peace, whom Solomon and all the Jewish kings typified in their royal
character.

Upon the birth of Solomon, the prophet Nathan
was sent to David, to inform him that the Divine favour rested upon this son, who also received the distinguished appellation of Jedidiah, or "the beloved of
the Lord," 2 Sam. xii. 25. He was about nineteen
years old when he succeeded his father as king of Israel;
and the Divine blessing had been promised, and was
vouchsafed to him in a remarkable degree. "The
Lord magnified Solomon exceedingly in the sight of all
Israel, and bestowed upon him such royal majesty as
had not been on any king before him in Israel,"
1 Chron. xxix. 25. He had to expect troubles from
the turbulent characters against whom his father had
cautioned him. The first proceeding of this nature was
shown by his brother Adonijah, who presented a request, through the queen-mother, that he might be permitted to marry Abishag, one of the secondary wives
of his father, whom David had taken in his old age,
but as an attendant, rather than as a wife. According
to the customs still prevalent in the east, this request
was in effect showing a determination to prosecute his
design to obtain the throne; for no private person might
marry the widow of a king; and, if the object were at-
tained, it would intimate that his pretensions to royalty
were well-founded. It was evident that a conspiracy
was formed by Joab and Abiathar, and the conduct of
these parties, when Solomon showed his determination
not to allow their proceedings to pass unnoticed, evinc-
ed consciousness of guilt. Adonijah thus brought punishment upon himself: if Solomon had desired his
death, Adonijah would have fallen at the moment the
new monarch ascended the throne—that is the period
when eastern despots sacrifice those whose existence

E

they fear. Abiathar, the priest, was spared, on account
of his sacred character, and his having shared in David's
troubles, but he was banished to Anathoth. Joab was
aware of the blood-guiltiness which had long pressed
upon him, as well as the treason he had lately been
contriving, and he attempted to shelter himself by flee-
ing to the tabernacle, where he caught hold on the
horns of the altar, as Adonijah had done, expecting
probably to be pardoned like him when he had thus
taken refuge ; but Solomon rightly decided, that the
sacred character of the house of God was not designed
to afford impunity to a criminal. Shimei's guilty conduct had been less notorious, and a farther trial was
granted him, but he was particularly restricted not to
leave Jerusalem, where he might be closely observed.
Three years after this, he broke the restriction by going
to Gath ; his intercourse with that place, so lately
brought under the Jewish rule, justly exposed him to
the punishment he received, and Solomon was then
freed from these dangerous enemies of his government.
His throne was established in peace ; his earliest measures included forming alliances of a friendly nature
with the neighbouring princes : there were no attempts
to find pretexts for quarrels or undue claims.

We now return to Solomon's accession. His first
care was to go to Gibeon, where the tabernacle, which
Moses had made in the wilderness, was then placed ;
there, on the brazen altar, associated with so many
recollections of the Divine goodness to Israel, Solomon
offered a thousand burnt offerings. This showed his
obedience to the ceremonial institutions, but we also
find that he prayed to Jehovah earnestly, in spirit and
in truth, humbly confessing that he was as a little child,
not knowing how to go out or come in. The Lord
heard his intercessions, and communicated with him by
a vision, engaging to grant the request he might make.
Solomon's petition was not for earthly good, but for an
understanding heart ; for the gift of Divine wisdom.
His prayer was granted, and a promise was added of

riches and honour, so that there should be no king like
him : the particulars are in 2 Chron. i. 7—12.   This
was soon manifested, as the history of Solomon proves.
An opportunity for judgment was presented before the
king, when he was enabled to ascertain the truth in a
very difficult matter, the contending claims of two mothers for a living infant ; and, by eliciting the feelings
of a mother for her child, he showed ability to discern,
where direct evidence could not be obtained.   And
he was careful in the administration of justice, acting
with impartiality towards the poor, as well as towards
the rich.   We must not omit to notice, that Solomon's
claims to authority are not founded on the visions at
Gibeon.   Numa, Mohammed, and other impostors, laid
claim to public support by pretending secret communications in visions ; but Solomon's authority rested on
other and more visible grounds.   The whole history
of Solomon proves that wisdom is better than might ; but
it is only Divine wisdom that will be found not to fail
in the time of difficulty, and in the hour of temptation.
Solomon sought the Divine blessing, and, in addition
to this, it was promised, that all things needful should
be added.

In 1 Kings iv. we read an account of the strength
and prosperity of Solomon's government, and the extent of his dominions, from the Mediterranean to the
Euphrates—from the Orontes to the Red Sea, and the
Persian Gulf ; but especially it is recorded, that he
" had peace on all sides round about him."   Happy
were the people that had such a prince to rule over
them !   A ·ruler who seeks to keep his subjects in
peace with other nations, does much to promote their
happiness and prosperity ; far more, than by waging
the most successful warfare.   Solomon was the type of
that glorious Prince, of whom the prophet Jeremiah
declares, " In his days Judah shall be saved, and Israel shall dwell safely : and this is his name whereby
he shall be called, The Lord our Righteousness," Jer.
xxiii. 6.   According to the prophetic words of Jacob,

Gen. xlix. 9, Judah, the reigning tribe, now couched
down as a lion, no nation ventured to rouse him up. At
that time the Hebrews were the ruling people in the
west of Asia.   David had laid the foundations of this
empire ; it prospered because he acted as viceroy to
the Almighty Power that condescended to rule over
Israel as a peculiar people.   If he had meditated foreign conquest by force of arms, the concluding judgment sent upon his government, taught both David
and his successor that this unhallowed passion must be
suppressed ; and the subsequent blessing upon the
peaceful rule of Solomon showed, that " when a man's
ways please the Lord, he maketh even his enemies to
be at peace with him," Prov. xvi. 7 ; and that kingdoms and empires may be obtained and preserved,
without the blood-stained laurels of the conqueror.
The scriptural account of Solomon's glory is plain and
decisive, and needs no confirmation ; the traditions
preserved in the poetical and legendary tales of Arabia,
may however be mentioned, as interesting documents
testifying to his power ; but they refer to spells and the
aid of demons, what the Bible simply and fully accounts
for by the measure of Divine wisdom imparted to Solomon, and the Divine blessing upon his proceedings.
We know that all may be done by the constraining influence of that Providence which guides and directs every
thing ; and we need not, with the followers of Mohammed, refer " to toiling genii," and " sounds that
burst the slumbers of the dead," the results of that
wisdom which cometh from above, which "is first pure,
then peaceable, full of mercy and good fruits."

The beautiful lines of Heber so well describe the
era which now rose upon Israel, that they may properly be inserted here,

For thee his ivory load behemoth bore,
And far Sofala teem'd with golden ore ;
Thine all the arts that wait on wealth's increase,
Or bask and wanton in the beam of peace.
When Tyber slept beneath the cypress gloom,
And silence held the lovely woods of Rome ;

Or ere to Greece the builder's skill was known,
Or the light chisel brush'd the Parian stone;
Yet here fair science nurs'd her infant fire,
Fann'd by the artist aid of friendly Tyre.
Then towered the palace, then in awful state
The temple rear'd its everlasting gate.

The temple was the first undertaking which engaged the attention of Solomon. He was directed to this, both by the charge of his dying father, and his own desire to construct a building for the solemn performance of the Divine services. In the needful preparations, the alliance of his father with Hiram, or Huram, king of Tyre, was of important service. Their correspondence at this time was sincere and cordial, to a degree seldom to be traced in the intercourse of the noble and powerful. It is given, 2 Chron. ii. 3—16.

" And Solomon sent to Huram the king of Tyre, saying, As thou didst deal with David my father, and didst send him cedars to build him an house to dwell therein, even so deal with me. Behold, I build an house to the name of the Lord my God, to dedicate it to him, and to burn before him sweet incense, and for the continual shewbread, and for the burnt offerings morning and evening, on the sabbaths, and on the new moons, and on the solemn feasts of the Lord our God. This is an ordinance for ever to Israel. And the house which I build is great : for great is our God above all gods. But who is able to build him an house, seeing the heaven and heaven of heavens cannot contain him ? who am I then, that I should build him an house, save only to burn sacrifice before him ? Send me now therefore a man cunning to work in gold, and in silver, and in brass, and in iron, and in purple, and crimson, and blue, and that can skill to grave with the cunning men that are with me in Judah and in Jerusalem, whom David my father did provide. Send me also cedar trees, fir trees, and algum trees, out of Lebanon : for I know that thy servants can skill to cut timber in Lebanon ; and, behold, my servants shall be with thy servants, even to prepare me timber in abundance : for the house which I am about to build shall be wonderful great. And, behold, I will give to thy servants, the hewers that cut timber, twenty thousand measures of beaten wheat, and twenty thousand measures of barley, and twenty thousand baths of wine, and twenty thousand baths of oil.

Then Huram the king of Tyre answered in writing, which he sent to Solomon, Because the Lord hath loved his people, he hath made thee king over them. Huram said moreover, Blessed be the Lord God of Israel, that made heaven and earth, who hath given to David the king a wise son, endued with prudence and understanding, that might build an house for the Lord, and an house for his kingdom. And now I have sent a cunning man, endued with understanding, of Huram my father's, the son of a woman of the daughters of Dan, and his father was a man of Tyre, skilful to work in gold, and in silver. in brass, in iron, in stone, and in timber, in purple, in blue, and in fine linen, and in crimson ; also to grave any manner of graving, and to find out every device which

E 2

shall be put to him, with thy cunning men, and with the cunning men of my lord David thy father. Now therefore the wheat, and the barley the oil, and the wine, whi. h my lord hath spoken of, let him send unto his servants: and we will cut wood out of Lebanon, as much as thou shalt need: and we will bring it to thee in flotes by sea to Joppa; and thou shalt carry it up to Jerusalem."

Hiram was a prince of a noble and liberal mind. Instead of evincing any mean jealousy at the rising greatness of Solomon, he gave him assistance, and permitted the Tyrians, then the most skilful artificers and mariners, to engage in the service of the Hebrew king. The forests of Lebanon alone could supply the cedars needed by Solomon; and the artizans of Sidon alone could execute the various kinds of workmanship. Large floats of timber were conveyed by sea to Joppa, and their value was paid by the agricultural produce of Judea. Ten thousand woodmen felled and squared timber in the mountain; at the end of a month they were relieved by others; and, after two months spent at home, they returned to their labour. Seventy thousand were carriers of burdens, and eighty thousand wrought in the quarries. These labourers were selected from the strangers in the land of Judea; chiefly the descendants of the Canaanites, who must in number have been half a million, and were now made regular tributaries to the king of Israel, engaged to render assigned portions of service; their employment in the erection of the temple was an indication that the Gentiles should eventually be included in the spiritual temple, the church of Christ.

The labour to prepare the site of the temple was very severe; the summit of the limestone rock of mount Moriah was levelled for the purpose. This spot had been purchased of Ornan, the Jebusite, by David, when directed by the prophet Gad to build there an altar to the Lord. As the area was not large enough to contain the building of the temple and its courts, a wall was built up from the valley beneath, constructed of immense masses of stone, firmly united together, and reaching to the stupendous height of

seven hundred feet. Let the reader imagine himself
standing in a narrow valley, and looking up towards
the top of an immense wall, more than half as high again
from the ground as St. Paul's cathedral, in London!
Much of this valley is now filled up, but the height
still is very great.

On the space thus obtained the temple was erected.
It was constructed on the plan of the tabernacle, but
enlarged, and with a number of small apartments, three
stories high, surrounding the principal pile, which in
some respects resembled a gothic church with a lofty
and broad tower in the front, and two low aisles on the
sides of the body. The accommodation for attendants,
and for stores and offerings, necessarily was considerable. This pile of building was surrounded by courts
for the worshippers. It was not so remarkable for size
or outward beauty, as for being constructed of the most
costly materials ; but the inside was carved and ornamented with much skill. The exceeding richness of
ornament, and the workmanship, rendered it the won-
der of the age in which it was erected, and no edifice
equal in these respects has since been constructed.
During seven years and a half this splendid fabric si-
lently but rapidly proceeded towards completion. Every
part and material of the building, even the largest beams
and the most ponderous stones, were fitted before they
were brought to the site.

> No workman's steel nor ponderous axes rung,
> Like some tall palm the noiseless fabric sprung.

In the work entitled, " THE RITES AND WORSHIP
OF THE JEWS," the reader will find a full account of the
temple and its courts, which our limits prevent us from
attempting to give in these pages. It certainly was
the most costly and magnificent building of which we
have any account in history. The time occupied in
completing the building was short, when the nature,
and extent, and variety of the work, as minutely described in sacred history, are considered. The alliance

of Hiram was very helpful to Solomon, and the brief
records of him, by ancient historians, show that he was
interested by the wisdom of the Jewish monarch. They
state, that he was much engaged in extensive buildings,
which would render his aid peculiarly valuable. This
aid from Hiram induced Solomon to forward the commercial enterprizes of the Tyrian prince. That the
latter sought to benefit from the power of Solomon, is
shown by the manner in which their joint enterprizes
were conducted from the ports of Edom; and by the
erection of frontier and outlying cities in positions
which facilitated trade, which will be noticed hereafter.
This may assist to explain the dissatisfaction expressed
by Hiram, when he saw the cities assigned to him by
Solomon in the land of Galilee. They were situated in
a fertile district, and would supply agricultural produce;
but they were not situated so as to facilitate the commercial enterprizes of Tyre. And a man immersed in
business, as in any other soul-engrossing pursuit, will
call every object worthless and displeasing that does
not forward his favourite views. The attention of Solomon was then directed to form stations, more likely
to promote the joint commercial enterprizes of the Tyrians and Hebrews.

When the temple was completed, it was dedicated
to the service of Jehovah, with much solemnity. All
Israel assembled for the occasion. The ark was borne
into the holy of holies by the Levites, and placed
within the vail. An immense number of sacrifices
were slain; they covered not only the new large brazen
altar, but also were piled in the middle of the court,
which formed one vast altar, requisite for the number
of victims on this occasion. And let us not forget, that
those victims were for the most part supplies of food
for the assembled multitude. How different from the
sacrifices of Roman emperors, a hundred lions, a hundred eagles, and a hundred swine!

The trumpeters and singers, and others with harps,
and psalteries, and cymbals, united in harmony. They

" made one sound to be heard in praising and thanking the Lord," saying, " For He is good; for his
mercy endureth for ever." The house was filled with
a cloud, the " glory of the Lord filled the house of
God." Psalms cxxxv. and cxxxvi. are thought to have
been recited on this occasion.

Solomon then ascended a stage or throne of brass,

placed in the midst of the court, and offered up the
beautiful prayer recorded 2 Chron. vi. and 1 Kings viii.
" The Lord hath said that he would dwell in the thick
darkness." In this prayer are most clear and powerful
recognitions of the omnipresence of the Lord, and his
providential care of his people. The special mercies
exhibited in behalf of Israel are remembered, and the
continuance of them implored, and that the Lord would
hear from heaven his dwelling place, when called upon
by sufferers in the land of captivity and affliction. " Behold, the heaven and the heaven of heavens cannot contain thee; how much less this house that I have builded! Hearken thou to the supplications of thy servant,
and of thy people Israel, when they shall pray toward
this place: and hear thou in heaven thy dwelling place;

and when thou hearest, forgive." How different this
language from that in which the heathens addressed
their gods, as tutelary deities of towns and provinces!
The prayer of Solomon, on this occasion, was at once
fervent and pathetic, solemn and full of humility. It
was the language of a sinner, laying himself in the dust
at the footstool of Divine mercy, acknowledging that
even his best performances were wholly unworthy of
the Divine regard. The reference to every man's
knowledge of the plague of his own heart, as essential
to enable him to offer real prayer and supplication, is
very beautiful and impressive. Sin is the plague of the
heart, this every true Israelite knows. The mention
of the stranger also shows the spiritual nature of the
worship to which Solomon referred, and that there was
Divine favour towards the Gentiles. A court for them
to worship in, formed a part of the buildings of the
temple. The conclusion *Hales* renders, " O Lord of
Gods, turn not away the face of thy Messiah; remember the mercies of David thy servant;" and remarks,
that Solomon could not apply the term Messiah, or the
Anointed, in this place, to himself; nor could he be
ignorant that it had been applied by his father David,
and by others, to the Son of God. How delightful to
see a king thus standing forth as the intercessor for his
people, and leading them in their prayers to God!
Solomon, on this occasion, appears to have been a type
of that Saviour who is the Intercessor for his people,
who pleads for them above.

> See through Him, the heavenly King,
> Who for his subjects prays!
> Israel's Intercessor sing,
> And magnify his grace :
> Praise our LORD, who ever lives
> To save and bless his saints forgiven,
> Till He to himself receives,
> And blesses us in heaven.

When this prayer was ended, fire was sent from
heaven, and consumed the burnt offerings and sacrifices ; the people bowed down upon the pavement, and

worshipped and praised the Lord, saying, "For He is good ; for his mercy endureth for ever." Solomon kept the feast of dedication seven days, and then concluded with a solemn assembly, doubtless engaging in spiritual worship, and sent the people to their homes, joyful in heart for the goodness the Lord had showed to David, to Solomon, and to all Israel. Several of the Psalms are supposed to have reference to this festival, as Psalms xlvii. xcvii. xcviii. and cvii. Psalm xxiv. probably was used on this occasion. The temple was a glorious structure ; the public service and the manifestation of the Divine splendour, were glorious ; but the vast multitude bowing as one man, and solemnly and joyfully acknowledging the Divine goodness, and imploring the Divine mercy, was a sight far more glorious. It was an anticipation of the yet more glorious assembly of the saints above. It was a year of jubilee, and the dedication of the temple was at a season especially appointed for sacred joy.

When the temple was completed, Solomon erected other buildings. His own palace was thirteen years in building ; it employed the utmost skill of the artificers of that day, and the vast resources of wealth and power at the command of Solomon ; but not a stone remains to tell where it stood, although masses, weighing several tons, were laid for the foundation, and built up in the walls. It was on Mount Zion, and communicated with the temple on Mount Moriah by a causeway across the ravine which separated those heights. The ranges of apartments were numerous and splendid, and were surrounded with beautiful gardens. Some consider that the house of the Forest of Lebanon was a part of the palace, probably forming a vast hall, 175 feet in length, wide and lofty in proportion, with a roof of cedar, from whence it received its appellation of " Lebanon." Others are of opinion that the house of the Forest of Lebanon was a country retirement ; and this may explain the use of the hall and judgment seat. At Jerusalem, the usual courts for the administration

of justice would suffice ; but, when the king was at
his country residence, it would be necessary that
courts for these purposes should be provided. From
one passage, it appears that Solomon had retirements
for pleasure in Lebanon itself ; and the rich variety of
scenery displayed among those mountains, with the
power of enjoying, in the space of a few miles, all the
changes of temperature and scenery displayed in every
region from the torrid to the frigid zones, rendered it
peculiarly suitable for the abode of such an observer of
nature, during his intervals of repose from the affairs
of state.

In the palace were porches or porticoes for judgment,
in one of which stood the great throne of ivory, over-
laid with the best gold ; sculptured lions ornamented
the six steps by which the king ascended to the seat of
the throne.   Another palace was built for the daughter of Pharaoh, the queen of Solomon, whom he married about the time of his accession ; but she was an
idolatress, and Solomon then feeling the evil of idolatry, would not bring her to reside in the house of David, for that place had been hallowed by the presence
of the ark.   The extent of Solomon's buildings is
mentioned by himself, Eccl. ii. 4—6, " I made me great
works ; I builded me houses ; I planted me vineyards :
I made me gardens and orchards, and I planted trees
in them of all kinds of fruits : I made me pools of
water, to water therewith the wood that bringeth forth
trees ;" and the particulars are largely described by *Josephus*. The only remains of these works which still exist are the pools of Solomon, situated to the south of
Bethlehem.   Perhaps among all the circumstances related of Solomon, none so deeply impress the youthful
mind with an idea of his earthly glory, as the details of
his palace and other buildings. *Josephus* says, " The
rooms were hung with rich hangings, and beautified with
images and sculptures of all kinds, exquisitely finished.
It would be an endless work to give a particular survey
of this splendid mass of building. So many courts,

such a variety of chambers and offices, galleries, vast rooms of state, and others for feasting and entertainment, set out richly with costly furniture and gilding ; and all the services for the king's table were of pure gold. The whole house was constructed of white marble, cedar, gold and silver, with precious stones upon the walls and ceilings." Thus we see the wealth and costliness of these structures, and that they were rapidly carried forward to completion by the vast resources at his command ; but in a few short years how changed the scene ! The mighty mind which directed their construction was soon exhibited in dotage, and the monarch became a tenant of the silent tomb, his honours possessed by an incapable successor, whose folly deprived him of the greater part of his power. Solomon, who erected these edifices, *himself* declares, " Then I looked on all the works that my hands had wrought, and on the labour that I had laboured to do ; and, behold, all was vanity and vexation of spirit !" And the experiences of the most successful of the sons of men, from that period to the present day, unanimously testify the same as to earthly affairs.

Other buildings of Solomon are enumerated, which were on a very extensive scale, towns and cities, with all their accompaniments : Gezer and Beth-horon in the south, and Baalbec in Syria, and Tadmor in the desert, or Palmyra, still magnificent in its ruins. These extensive erections must have absorbed vast sums, and though at first executed by the strangers in the land, yet in the end the people of Israel were compelled to assist, both by payment of taxes, and by personal services ; and these probably were some of the causes of that discontent which deprived Solomon's successor of his father's power. Descending to private life, it is remarkable how often we find the ruin of individuals, and the destruction of families, connected with large proceedings in building, and unwillingness to rest satisfied with the ample blessings sent directly to us. Another serious source of expense was the establishments for horses.

F

These were on a very large scale, and engrossed much
attention. *Josephus* describes both the horses and their
riders as incomparable. The former were noted for
their beauty and swiftness, the latter were selected for
their stature and comeliness. They were clothed in
purple, and their hair was powdered with gold-dust,
which glittered in the sun. This passion for cavalry
was contrary to the Divine injunction, and tended to
promote intercourse with Egypt, which was strictly
forbidden by the word of God.

The vast treasures needed for Solomon's works
were supplied from various sources. A large part was
derived from commerce, as the trade of the civilized
world then almost entirely passed under the control of
Solomon and Hiram ; and while the latter furnished
merchants and seamen, the former supplied all the
stores needed, from the resources of an agricultural
country. Trade, at that period, was not conducted by
individual enterprize, the profits were not subject to
much competition, nor divided among a number of ad-
venturers. All was conducted under the authority of
the monarch, and a large proportion of the advantages
remained in his coffers. It was at a later period that
the prophet spoke of the merchants of Tyre as princes.
The foreign trade of the confederate kings of Judea
and Tyre, probably, extended through the Mediterranean Sea to the western coasts of Africa, and even to
the British Islands. In the opposite direction, by the
Red Sea : the shores of eastern Africa, and of India,
were visited by their fleets ; for which purpose the
port of Eziongeber, near Elath, in the country of Edom,
was selected by Solomon, and vessels were constructed
expressly for these voyages. The Jewish monarch occupied the ports, and garrisoned the country of Idumea,
but the king of Tyre found the ship-builders and the
sailors, and probably was the projector of the enterprize. An inland trade from Egypt on the south, for
linen and horses, through Judea to Syria and other
countries to the north and to the east, left considerable

profits to Solomon ; in addition to those resulting from
" the spice merchants," the Arabian caravans which

traversed his dominions, carrying all the precious commodities of the east ; and they still pursue a similar
route.   To these may be added, the line of caravans
proceeding directly across Asia, from the Euphrates and
Babylon, to Tyre, as a protection for which Solomon
was induced to build the city of Palmyra.   All the nations and tribes surrounding Judea, whether wild or civilized, whether ancient enemies of the people of God,
or those to whom his former dealings were unknown,
alike owned the sway of Solomon, though he sought not
to dazzle or terrify the nations, by arms ; the value of
his alliance was recognized, and his friendship was
sought.   But though so powerful, and so highly endued
with wisdom, Solomon's royal authority was limited ;
he had a written law, divinely inspired, from which he
could not depart without bringing guilt and suffering
upon himself.   The Jewish princes were strictly bound
to maintain the law as given by Moses, and we must
observe, that trade and conquest are not primary objects encouraged by that code.

Judea itself was a fruitful country ; rendered so by

the Divine blessing upon the simple industry of the
people, during a longer period of internal peace, under
Solomon and his predecessors, than had been known
since they possessed the land. This state of peace
and plenty is figuratively, but expressively described
in the words, "Judah and Israel dwelt safely, every man
under his vine, and under his fig-tree, from Dan even
unto Beersheba, all the days of Solomon." The precious metals may be dug from the earth, and enrich
the finder, but the general wealth of a community
must be drawn from the surface, and, doubtless, at this
time Judea yielded a larger return to the tillers' toil
than ever before or since.

Again we would say, that the great instrumental
cause of all Solomon's advantages, under the Divine
blessing, was the wisdom which God put into his
heart. "There came of all people to hear the wisdom
of Solomon, from all kings of the earth, which had
heard of his wisdom." Among these monarchs, the
queen of Sheba is especially noticed ; the "queen of
the South," as she is called by our Lord. She had
heard of the wisdom of Solomon, and came to prove
him with hard questions, matters of difficulty on which
information was required, and probably also the " dark
sayings," or enigmas, so highly esteemed in the east ;
to the proposing and the resolving of which much importance is attached, even by kings and princes at the
present day. Solomon was enabled to answer, so that
the queen declared it was a true report she had heard
in her own land of his acts and wisdom ; fame had
not exaggerated the particulars ; and she added, that
even the half was not told. " Happy are these thy servants which stand continually before thee, and that
hear thy wisdom. Blessed be the Lord thy God,
which delighteth in thee, to set thee on the throne of
Israel ; because the Lord loved Israel for ever, therefore made he thee king, to do judgment and justice."
She returned to her own country, probably in the
southern district of Arabia, after presenting the king

with a large amount of gold and other valuable commodities.   Other kings and great men, who sent and
resorted to Solomon, offered largely, and all tended to
the temporal advantage of himself and his people, so
that "the king made silver to be in Jerusalem as
stones, and cedars to be as the sycamore trees that
are in the vale, for abundance."   The plentiful supply
of the precious metals which existed in ancient times,
was proved by the remains of two ancient vessels
which were discovered sunk in the harbour of Cartha-
gena, in Spain ; the bottoms were covered with plates
of silver, in the same manner that copper is used at
the present day.   Gold, ever reckoned the most precious metal, was then yielded largely in many parts of
the east, by rivers and other spots which have been ran-
sacked and cleared of their golden stores ages since.
But as to the pomp and magnificence of Solomon,
let us remember the words of our blessed Lord, who,
pointing to the lilies of the field, abounding as weeds
in eastern countries, solemnly declared, "that even
Solomon in all his glory was not arrayed like one of
these ;" Matt. vi. 29.   And as we shall see when we
notice the book of Ecclesiastes, all this earthly pomp
and wealth could afford no real satisfaction.

The wisdom of Solomon was beyond that of any
other mortal ;

> ———————— his mighty mind,
> Through nature's mazes wander'd unconfin'd ;
> He every bird, and beast, and insect knew,
> And spake of every plant that quaffs the dew.

Or, as the simple, yet energetic language of Scripture
expresses, " He spake of trees, from the cedar that
was in Lebanon, even unto the hyssop that springeth
out of the wall : he spake also of beasts, and of fowl,
and of creeping things, and of fishes."   But his wisdom more particularly referred to spiritual knowledge,
to that which is good for the soul.   He spake three

thousand proverbs, a portion of which remain in the book called by that name.

What an extensive and excellent system of ethics is here set forth! and the christian reader will bear testimony that the promise is fulfilled. Take the proverbs of other nations, and we shall find numbers are founded upon selfishness, cunning, pride, injustice, national contempt, and public or private animosities. But the principles of the proverbs of Solomon are piety, charity, justice, benevolence, and true prudence. Their universal purity proves their inspiration. The heart and life of man is laid open, and characters of every rank and nation, from the time when they were first spoken, to the consummation of all things, are addressed.

Another portion of the extraordinary gifts possessed by Solomon is shown by his Divine songs. These were a thousand and five. Only a few remain in the Book of Canticles—a portion of holy writ often misrepresented by worldly minds, and often misunderstood by those who are more correctly disposed towards Divine things. With respect to misrepresentations, these, when not wilful, may arise from ignorance of the spirit and meaning of oriental poetry, and a want of acquaintance with eastern manners and customs. This latter circumstance has materially affected our English version, so that in many passages the English reader has a very different meaning conveyed to his mind, from that which is received by a person aequainted with the original. The misunderstanding as to this book arises from various causes ; the primary reference may be to the daughter of Pharaoh, or, as is more probable, to a variety of pastoral subjects ; but there can be no just doubt that it is parabolical, and like the parables spoken by our Lord, it is to be applied to illustrate some important truth ; and in this book, the love of Christ for his church, and the affection manifested towards him by his faithful people are evidently set forth.

Some may carry the allegory too far, and enter too minutely into detail, but the ground-work cannot be mistaken. It is similar to the language employed in many other places of holy writ, as Psalm xlv., various passages of the prophets, and even the words of our blessed Lord himself; see Matt. ix. 15; xxv. 1. This book has a peculiar and internal meaning, very different from that of any other eastern poem. It admits of mystical interpretation, with a consistency which cannot be found to apply to any uninspired poem; and though every christian may not derive equal profit therefrom, yet thousands have been strengthened and supported by its contents in the hour of trial, and have had their devout affections increased thereby.

We may regret the loss of a considerable part of the writings of Solomon, but we may be assured, that all which are desirable for spiritual instruction have been preserved. And in reference to other portions of his works which have not come down to us, the whole of Solomon's maxims, and the whole of his poetry might not be Divinely inspired; and the account of the animal and vegetable tribes might be rather a philosophical than a religious work. Others, doubtless, were the enigmatical and dark sayings, which the wise and learned of the east occupy themselves so frequently in proposing and solving. *Josephus* expressly states, that much of the correspondence between Hiram and Solomon was of this nature, and the "hard questions" proposed by the queen of Sheba have already been noticed. Much is said in eastern books of the writings of Solomon, and many fables are related concerning them; these are unworthy of notice, as also are the legendary tales of the rabbins respecting this mighty prince. One specimen of their exaggerations will suffice. They represent that on the right side of his throne were twelve thousand seats for patriarchs and prophets, and on the left twelve thousand for doctors of the law, who assisted in administering justice. What consultations could be carried on, what justice could

be administered in such an assembly? Yet there is
no doubt that ingenious and learned men lived at Jerusalem in the reign of Solomon, and under his pa-
tronage. Among them probably were Ethan the
Ezrahite, and Heman, and Chalcol and Darda, the sons
of Mahol, mentioned 1 Kings iv. 31. Their conferences
may be noticed, Eccl. xii. 11. The apocryphal book
called " The Wisdom of Solomon," evidently was the
work of a writer of later date.

When Solomon had finished his own palace, and
the other works which occupied him till about the
twentieth year of his reign, the Lord again communicated with him by vision, and repeated his promise to
bless his sanctuary, and to hear and answer prayer.
The strongest promises of confirming his throne were
made, if he would walk in the ways of his father David, and observe the Divine statutes and judgments ;
but, on the other hand, a warning of punishment was
sent, if he or his successors forsook the statutes and
commandments of the Lord, 2 Chron. vii. 12—22.
This may be considered as a solemn declaration of the
consequences that would follow his disobedience.

The arrangements of Solomon for the support of the
state and magnificence which his prosperity led him to
assume, were regularly organized, and efficient ; though
they cannot be fully appreciated by those who are
only acquainted with European manners, and modern
customs. The details preserved respecting later eastern monarchs show a similar provision, and on a scale
proportionably large. The particulars are given in
1 Kings iv. The land was divided into twelve districts,
not according to the divisions of the tribes, but probably
arranged by an average of the fertility of the land, for
from each, in succession, provision was supplied for a
month. And of the officers who managed these affairs,
it is recorded, what never could be said of the ministers
of any other earthly prince, that they provided so that
nothing was lacked. While the Divine blessing rested
on the king, it is evident that the people were happy ;

and this provision was made without oppressive exactions. The supply for each day was 30 measures, or 280 bushels of fine flour, and twice that quantity of meal ; 30 oxen and 100 sheep, besides other animals. This large supply of provision is calculated by some to be enough for 50,000 persons ; and it must be remembered, that the visitors to Solomon were numerous, and their retinues large. Also it shows the largeness of Solomon's court, which, besides officers and guards, included 700 wives, princesses of various nations, and 300 of lower rank. This part of his state, the multiplication of wives, was the source of much evil, and he himself records, that he did not find among them one deserving of confidence, Eccl. vii. 28. It has been well remarked, how could this be expected among the characters Solomon chose ? And he declares, "favour is deceitful, and beauty is vain ; but a woman that feareth the Lord, she shall be praised." These idolatrous women turned away his heart, so that he went after the idols they worshipped. He not only allowed them to erect places for themselves to worship idols, but he burned incense and sacrificed with them. This most awful delusion, it is calculated, took place about the 34th year of his reign, and the 54th of his age. Perhaps there is not a more striking instance of the natural depravity of man's heart recorded in Scripture, and it is not only a warning to those of exalted station, like Solomon, but to those of every rank. It is not only a warning against that besetting sin by which Solomon fell, but it speaks to every one that standeth, to take heed lest he fall, by whatever temptation assailed.

If the history of Solomon is examined, it will be found that his fall was by degrees. How painful to consider, that the words spoken by him were not applicable to his own case ; "the hoary head is a crown of glory, if it be found in the way of righteousness!" Prov. xvi. 31 ; and still more painful is it to find that one so well acquainted with the deceitfulness of the human heart, was so blind as to the depravity of his own. The

extensive outward advantages he possessed were not
enjoyed with simple devotedness to the Giver. How
needful the prayer, " In all time of our wealth deliver
us, O Lord!"

A solemn denunciation was made to Solomon, that
the kingdom should be rent from his family ; not indeed
all the kingdom, one tribe should be left, Judah and
Benjamin were now united, Jerusalem being situated
partly in each ; this was for the sake of David, and for
the sake of Jerusalem : God's sparing mercies have
often been continued to a nation for the sake of his
church. A direct communication to the same effect
was soon afterwards made by the prophet Ahijah to
Jeroboam, a man of Ephraim, whom Solomon appointed
ruler over the house or family of Joseph, or superin-
tendent of those from among that people employed on
public works in Jerusalem. As a sign, the prophet rent
his own new garment into twelve pieces, giving ten of
them to Jeroboam ; but a plain intimation was added,
that David was not rejected as Saul had been. His
family should be continued, as the Messiah was to proceed from him, and though afflicted with captivities, it
should not perish for ever. Solomon's deplorable fall
is farther shown by his endeavour to kill Jeroboam, although he had taught, that whatever may be the devices in the heart of man, still the counsel of the Lord
shall stand. Of course, his wicked design was disappointed ; Jeroboam fled to Egypt, and found an asylum
there. The alliance with Egypt, which caused so much
evil to Solomon, had ended in disappointment ; the
particulars are not related, but when we find the oppo-
nent of Solomon sheltered there, it is manifest, that, like
his successors, he found that confidence in Egyptian
fidelity was leaning on a broken reed. Two foreign
adversaries also appeared against Solomon, Hadad of
Edom, and Rezon the ruler of Damascus, but they did
not proceed to open hostilities during the life of Solomon. At the beginning of his reign he was able to
write to Hiram, that no one appeared as an adversary

against him ; but now, when he had departed from the
ways of the Lord, three were at once raised up as his
opponents. See 1 Kings xi.

And did this mighty king, the wisest of men, find satisfaction in his earthly pursuits and sensual pleasures ?
and did he die in his sin ? To the first question we
can reply decidedly, that he did *not* find rest for his
soul in any earthly good, though pursued by him with
greater opportunities and facilities for enjoyment, than
by any other of the sons of men. The book of Ecclesiastes is a valuable record of his experience ; every
sort of gratification, connected with the lust of the
flesh, the lust of the eyes, and the pride of life, is enumerated in succession, and declared to be utterly worthless, altogether disappointing. All was found to be
" vanity and vexation of spirit ;" " vanity of vanities,
all is vanity." In like manner the votaries of pleasure
of later days are compelled to come to the same conclusion, and when speaking of the worldly gratifications
and sensual enjoyments of a long life, they are con-
strained to confess, that they "by no means desire to
repeat the nauseous dose, for the sake of its fugitive
dream." But the christian, however harassed by outward trials or inward temptations, does not speak thus
of life—not even of the poor perishing life of this
world. Youthful reader! form a right estimate of life.
The apostle could say, "to me to live is Christ, and to
die is gain."

In Ecclesiastes there is free and full argumentation
upon the questions introduced. Whatever can be al-
leged in support of seeking gratification in the things
of time and sense is fully examined. It is not a que-
rulous detail of disappointment, but the question is de-
liberately and carefully investigated. And Solomon
does not speak only in a condemnatory strain of earthly
gratifications ; he declares God hath made every thing
beautiful in its time, and appointed man to rejoice in
his mercies, and to enjoy them as the gift of God.
Yes, reader, we do live in a beautiful world ; look

around, and behold all the glorious objects of creation ;
see the comforts God has permitted the heart of man
to devise, and the lawful enjoyments he permits him to
possess, and then say,

These are thy glorious works, Parent of good.

And add—

> O God ! O good beyond compare!
> If thus thy meaner works are fair,
> If thus thy beauties gild the span
> Of ruined earth and sinful man,
> How glorious must the mansion be
> Where thy redeemed shall dwell with Thee!

The book of Ecclesiastes also calls attention to futurity ; it shows that God will judge the righteous and the
wicked ; and that there is a solemn and all-important difference between the spirit of a man, and the spirit of a
beast. Solomon meets the libertine on his own ground ;
he tells him to rejoice, if he pleases, in the ways of his
heart, and in the sight of his eyes ; but to *know* that
for all these things God will bring him into judgment.
He counsels us from his own experience, to "remember
the Creator in the days of youth," and not to think
that a late repentance may be granted, or will suffice.
He directs to the one Shepherd as the Giver of wisdom ;
and he ends with a solemn warning : "Let us hear the
conclusion of the whole matter : Fear God, and keep
his commandments : for this is the whole duty of man,
his chief and only good. "For God shall bring every
work into judgment, with every secret thing ; whether
it be good, or whether it be evil."

As this book evidently was the production of the
latter days of Solomon, we are warranted to hope and
believe, that he died sincerely penitent, and restored
to the Divine favour. But let us learn from his example to avoid sin and folly : and since no account of his
latter hours is given—since we have no express record
of his repentance, let us beware how we trifle with our
mercies. And if we have erred and strayed from the
paths of righteousness and peace, let us, as we hope

Solomon did, return from the broken and empty cisterns of this world to the Fountain of living waters ; and, like the Jewish monarch, let us warn others not to go on in the paths of danger, lest we die therein.

Theh istory of Solomon is well summed up by the Jewish author of Ecclesiasticus. "Solomon reigned in a peaceable time, and was honoured ; for God made all quiet about him, that he might build a house to his name, and prepare his sanctuary for ever. How wise wast thou in thy youth, and, as a flood, filled with understanding! Thy soul covered the whole earth, and thou filledst it with dark parables. Thy name went far unto the islands ; and for thy peace thou wast beloved. The countries marvelled at thee for thy songs, and proverbs, and parables, and interpretations. By the name of the Lord God, which is called the Lord God of Israel, thou didst gather gold as tin, and didst multiply silver as lead. Thou didst give thyself unto women, and by thy body thou wast brought into subjection. Thou didst stain thine honour, so that thou broughtest wrath upon thy children, and wast grieved for thy folly ; so the kingdom was divided, and a hard tyranny set up in Ephraim. But the Lord will never cease from mercy, neither shall any of his works perish, neither will he abolish the posterity of his elect, and the seed of him that loveth him he will not take away ; wherefore he gave a remnant unto Jacob, and out of him a root unto David. Thus rested Solomon with his fathers."

REHOBOAM.

REIGNED OVER JUDAH SEVENTEEN YEARS.

[B. C. 990—973.]

SOLOMON left but one son ; two daughters are mentioned, Basmath and Taphath. The latter were married to two of the officers enumerated in 1 Kings iv., to

G

whom pertained the duty of providing for the king and
his court. The son was Rehoboam, whose mother
was Naamah, an Ammonitess; he must have been born
in the year that his father came to the throne, as he
was himself forty-one years old when he began to reign.
Therefore, during all the time Solomon was king of
Israel, he had his successor in view, and doubtless endeavoured to render him worthy to sit upon the throne
of David. How great must have been his disappointment in Rehoboam! We have not to infer this merely
from the character of the latter, as displayed on his accession to the throne. The disappointment appears to
be recorded by Solomon himself; "And I turned myself to behold wisdom, and madness, and folly. (For
what can the man do that cometh after the king?
even that which hath been already done.) Then I
saw that wisdom excelleth folly, as far as light excelleth darkness. The wise man's eyes are in his head;
but the fool walketh in darkness: and I myself perceived also that one event happeneth to them all. Then
said I in my heart, As it happeneth to the fool, so it
happeneth even to me; and why was I then more
wise! Then I said in my heart, that this also is vanity."
Eccl. ii. 12—15. He uses still stronger expressions;
"Yea, I hated all my labour which I had taken under
the sun: because I should leave it unto the man that
shall be after me. And who knoweth whether he shall
be a wise man or a fool? yet shall he have rule over all
my labour wherein I have laboured, and wherein I have
showed myself wise under the sun:—this is also vanity!
Therefore I went about to cause my heart to despair
of all the labour which I took under the sun. For there
is a man whose labour is in wisdom, and in knowledge,
and in equity; yet to a man that hath not laboured
therein shall he leave it for his portion:—this also is
vanity and a great evil," verses 18—21. Also Eccl. x.
14—17, and xi. 9, 10, seem to imply a painful feeling
with regard to his successor; and it is not easy to
fix upon any passage in the writings of Solomon,

which can be understood as expressing satisfaction
respecting his son, or implying that the heir-apparent
was a praiseworthy character. Dark must have been
the prospects of the Jewish nation under such circumstances; and the conduct of Rehoboam probably gave
Solomon no reason to hope well of the future character of the son that was to succeed him.

When matters go wrong upon one point of importance, any predisposition to evil which may have existed on other grounds will be brought forward. It
was thus in the land of Palestine. From the early days
of the settlement of the Jewish nation, an envious feeling had existed between the sons of Ephraim and the
sons of Judah. The pre-eminence obtained by the
latter tribe had been displeasing to the others; and Solomon's conduct in his declining years, unpopular, and
in some respects oppressive, irritated these feelings.
The assembling of the tribes at Shechem, and their resolving to propose conditions to the new king, implies
that Solomon had departed from the covenant made
with David.

One source of this discontent is plainly stated—the
number of idolatrous wives of the late monarch had led
to many proceedings grievous to true Israelites, from
their direct influence upon Solomon, and from the
charge of an establishment so numerous and so expen-
sive. The tribes, however, seem to have been inclined
to obey the son of Solomon as their king, but they required from him a pledge that less oppressive measures should be adopted. They sent for Jeroboam, who
was then an exile in Egypt, to be their spokesman on
this occasion, and it is very probable that some had already determined to have him for their ruler. This
was the will of God, who was pleased to make use of
these unruly spirits to fulfil his threat to Solomon, and
the promise to Jeroboam.

Rehoboam took time to consider what answer he
should return, but he showed the natural bent of his
mind, by rejecting the advice his father's counsellors

gave, and by following that of the young men who
were his favourites and companions. The folly of such

a course is so obvious, that when it is remembered that
Rehoboam was at this time forty years of age, we at
once form a decided judgment respecting his character.
His conduct proceeded from an infatuation which, as
Scripture informs us, was made instrumental in accom-
plishing the Lord's will. Surely this should warn every
one, whatever his rank and station, not to listen to
flatterers, or to think that pleasant companions make
the best advisers; and it is a caution not to throw away
our spiritual advantages by our own folly.

The leaders of the tribes at once determined on their
course; they renounced all allegiance to a son of David,
and resolved to separate from the tribe of Judah. Rehoboam made bad worse, by endeavouring to enforce
his unpopular measures by Adoram, the very person
whose conduct had been remonstrated against, who was
over the tribute. This officer was stoned, and Rehoboam hastened from Shechem to Jerusalem, when Je-

roboam was chosen as king by all the tribes, excepting Judah and Benjamin, to which Philistia and Edom were now attached. These districts remained faithful as tributaries to Rehoboam, who with the same hasty presumption that characterized his previous conduct, called forth all who were able to bear arms, meaning to attempt the subjugation of the other tribes by force; but Shemaiah, a prophet, was commissioned to rebuke the king of Judah, and to dismiss the multitude assembled to fight against Israel.

Jeroboam was thus made ruler over the largest part of the nation of the Jews ; but he felt insecure on his throne, and he was particularly apprehensive that if his subjects went up to Jerusalem to worship at the appointed festivals, they would be inclined to unite with their brethren, and support the house of David. He, therefore, resolved to introduce a new religious system throughout the ten tribes. He instituted a ritual, and constituted objects for worship, which retained some reference to Jehovah, acknowledging his mercies to the nation, and using forms similar to the worship of the ceremonial law of the land ; while, instead of Jerusalem, Bethel in the centre, and Dan in the north, were appointed as places for sacrifice ; and instead of the temple and the ark, two " calves" of gold, perhaps images having the cherubic form, were set up at the places for worship. These might in some respects have been derived from the forms of Egyptian worship, which the new king witnessed while an exile in that country ; but it is probable that the images were, in the first instance, only represented as symbols to direct and assist the people in the worship of Jehovah. Such representations, however intended, or however explained, always lead to idolatry, and this was the case with Jeroboam's idols—when calves, or cherubs, were set up as visible objects for worship, Baal and Ashtaroth soon were introduced.

False religions require ministers of a similar spirit. Many priests and Levites refused this worship ; they

G 2

were driven from Israel, and took refuge in Judah, while from " the lowest of the people," men without knowledge or piety, priests were appointed ; and festivals differing from those commanded in the law were instituted. To encourage his people in these practices, Jeroboam himself officiated as a priest at the altar which he had made, when a remarkable warning was sent to check his evil ways. A prophet arrived from Judah, and denounced the destruction of that pile, by a king of the family of David, who would be named Josiah, and gave a sign which was immediately fulfilled, thus satisfying the beholders that, according to the word he was sent to declare, the worship established by Jeroboam would be done away, while the worship appointed by the Lord should continue. The altar was shaken by an invisible power, and the fire and the sacrifices were scattered from it ; the arm of Jeroboam which he stretched forth, commanding that the prophet should be seized, withered, and lost all power. The king humbled himself so far, as to intreat the prophet to pray that his arm might be restored ; but he did not desire that his heart should be changed, nor humble himself for his transgression, whereby he made Israel to sin.

Yet Jeroboam was touched by this manifestation of mercy, he desired the prophet to accompany him to his home, and receive a reward. But this was forbidden. The prophet of Judah was to bear testimony against the idolatrous rites of Israel, and not to expose himself to the temptation of idolatrous pleasures. He left Bethel, refusing any reward, declaring that he was forbidden even to eat or drink. But, wearied and spent, he rested by the way-side, and he presently listened to the false statement of an old prophet, an inhabitant of Bethel, who followed him, pretending to have received a message from God, contradicting the command previously given to the true prophet, and inviting his return. The man of God, forgetting that the Lord would not contradict his own word, listened

to the temptation, and returned to the forbidden feast.
Being there Divinely warned, he again departed,
mounted on an ass belonging to his treacherous host,
but he had not gone far before he was slain by a lion ;
the animal showing that although the prophet had forgotten the limited extent of his commission, a wild beast

did not forget ; for it remained by the dead body without tearing the corpse, or destroying the ass on which
the prophet rode.   The whole narrative is very important, and shows that nothing can justify or excuse
disobedience to the Divine command.   It warns the
pastor, as well as the flock, not to trifle with the Divine
precepts, nor to point out the way without pursuing
it stedfastly.

Though a double seal was thus put to the Divine
warning, Jeroboam persisted in his idolatrous course,
and this piece of state policy, intended to secure his
government and that of his family, we are expressly
told was the cause for which they were cut off,
1 Kings xiii. 34.   We are to remember, that the government of Israel was always connected with the immediate superintendence and direction of· Jehovah,
and that Divine providence was propitious or adverse
to these nations, as their kings, the viceroys of the
Theocracy, or Divine government, adhered to the
will of God, or were opposed thereto.   The fate of
Jeroboam's family showed this result, even in the
early days of the divided kingdoms.

Rehoboam, being restrained from efforts to recover

the ten tribes, took measures for strengthening his
kingdom.   He received the priests and Levites who
were driven from the revolted districts, and others
who set their hearts to seek the Lord God of Israel.
There have been some in every age, who have willingly given up their worldly advantages to secure
advantages for their souls.   Such refugees ever bring
a blessing with them, and a curse will fall upon those
who drive them out.   Rehoboam continued to follow
these good courses three years, but then he gave
himself up to his pleasures, and the people began to
adopt the idolatries of neighbouring nations, and the
abominations of the old inhabitants of the land.   The
declension was rapid and general, but the Lord had
purposes of mercy for Judah, and he speedily sent
chastisement.   Shishak, the king of Egypt, finding the
Jews weakened and divided, came up with a great host
from the various nations of his empire, and the fortified
cities of Judah fell before him.   Shemaiah, the prophet,
declared to Rehoboam and the princes the cause of
these judgments, and they humbled themselves before
the Lord.   Their repentance was accepted, and though
made subject to Shishak, he was not permitted to
destroy them, but returned home loaded with the spoil
of the palace and temple of Jerusalem.   This conqueror afterwards built a large palace at Carnac, in
Egypt, where, in the year 1828, a sculpture on a
ruined wall was discovered, upon which is portrayed
the victor dragging thirty captive chiefs.   One has in
hieroglyphics upon his shield, *Jodaha Malek*, that is,
" the king of Judah."

After this chastisement Rehoboam was more obe-
dient to the word of the Lord, and we read that in
Judah there were yet good things ; some, doubtless,
were made better by the calamities of their country,
and others were thereby restrained from growing worse.
Rehoboam kept up the form of devotion more strictly,
and endeavoured to supply the place of the splendid
articles which had been removed, by others of an in-

ferior description. His golden shields were gone, but
he provided shields of brass. Is not this, in one sense,
often the case ; when we lose sight of the fine gold,
the precious promises, do not we often seek to supply
their place by what may bear some outward resem-
blance thereto, though wholly destitute of " the fine
gold" of the Divine word ?

Rehoboam died after a reign of seventeen years,
passed mostly in petty warfare with Jeroboam. He left
a numerous issue. It may be remarked here, that frequent mention is made of the mothers of the kings ;
but this is thought not always to denote their own
mothers, but one of the wives of the late king, who
was honoured with the title of queen-mother, a rank
still retained in eastern kingdoms. But we read that
the mother of Rehoboam was an Ammonitess, not one
of the people of Jehovah, 2 Chron. xii. 13 ; and the
next words expressly tell us, that he did evil, because
he prepared not, or, as the margin renders, he fixed
not his heart to seek the Lord. No word of Scripture is written without a meaning ; may not this be
intended to declare the inestimable value of a pious
mother ? History records many examples which prove
this : Solomon himself knew the value of a pious mother, but he knew it not till it was too late to secure a
like advantage for his son ! Let the sons of God be
careful how they take to themselves wives of the
daughters of men, whom they may be inclined to
choose. Of what vast, what unspeakable importance,
that the children of a family should have a mother
whom they may call blessed, who never will let her
eye rest on the infant upon her bosom without offering
a prayer, that she may not be bringing up a child that
shall be a servant of Satan ! How important that,
from its earliest years, a child should be taught the
necessity of deciding whether it will serve the Lord
Jesus Christ, or the great enemy of souls ! The apostle writes, that " a double-minded man is unstable in
all his ways," and Rehoboam was one of this class.

See page 72.

ABIJAM, or ABIJAH.

REIGNED THREE YEARS.

[B. C. 973—970.]

IN pursuing this history, we note the periods by the reigns of the kings of Judah. They were the sons of David, to whom the Lord had assured the kingdom, see 2 Sam. vii. 12—16 ; and although the Lord chastened his descendants with the rod of men, when they committed iniquity, and suffered his people to be divided between two rulers, yet the kingdom was with the sons of David, and the others were opposers of the Divine covenant in this matter. The main course of our narrative will, therefore, rest with the kings of Judah, but the monarchs of Israel will all be noticed according to the periods in which they reigned.

Abijah was the son of Rehoboam, by his favorite wife Maachah, a descendant of Absalom. Immedi-

ately after his accession to the throne, he called out
the forces of Judah to war against Israel. The aggres-
sor is not distinctly marked, but the main battle was
fought in the tribe of Ephraim. The king of Judah addressed his army in powerful and pious language.

" And Abijah stood up upon mount Zemaraim, which is in mount
Ephraim, and said, Hear me, thou Jeroboam, and all Israel ; Ought
ye not to know that the Lord God of Israel gave the kingdom over Israel
to David for ever, even to him and to his sons by a covenant of salt?
Yet Jeroboam the son of Nebat, the servant of Solomon the son of David,
is risen up, and hath rebelled against his lord. And there are gathered
unto him vain men, the children of Belial, and have strengthened
themselves against Rehoboam the son of Solomon, when Rehoboam
was young and tender-hearted, and could not withstand them. And
now ye think to withstand the kingdom of the Lord in the hand of the
sons of David ; and ye be a great multitude, and there are with you
golden calves, which Jeroboam made you for gods. Have ye not cast
out the priests of the Lord, the sons of Aaron, and the Levites, and have
made you priests after the manner of the nations of other lands ? so
that whosoever cometh to consecrate himself with a young bullock and
seven rams, the same may be a priest of them that are no gods. But as
for us, the Lord is our God, and we have not forsaken him ; and the
priests, which minister unto the Lord, are the sons of Aaron, and the
Levites wait upon their business : and they burn unto the Lord every
morning and every evening burnt sacrifices and sweet incense : the
shewbread also set they in order upon the pure table ; and the candle-
stick of gold with the lamps thereof, to burn every evening : for we
keep the charge of the Lord our God ; but ye have forsaken him. And,
behold, God himself is with us for our captain, and his priests with
sounding trumpets to cry alarm against you. O children of Israel,
fight ye not against the Lord God of your fathers ; for ye shall not
prosper." 2 Chron xiii. 4—12.

The men of Israel were defeated with great slaughter,
and a part of the land was subjected to Abijah. We
are expressly told, " Thus the children of Israel were
brought under at that time, and the children of Judah
prevailed, because they relied upon the Lord God of
their fathers." Yet Abijah's heart was not right with
the Lord ; his reign was short : three years after his
accession he died, and Jeroboam survived him in
Israel only two years longer. Another event of the
reign of the latter is related. His eldest son falling
sick, he sent his wife to the prophet Ahijah, who first
announced to him that he should be raised to kingly
power. She went, feigning herself to be a common
person, to inquire whether her afflicted son would

recover, and carried a present of bread, and cakes, and
honey, suitable to her assumed rank ; but though Ahijah was blind, he was enabled to detect the imposture.
He was Divinely warned of her approach, and on her
entrance greeted her as the wife of Jeroboam, with
heavy tidings of the death of her child, and of the destruction of her family. But the removal of her son
in peace was declared to be an act of mercy, because
there was found in him some good thing towards the
Lord God of Israel. She returned home, and as she
entered the palace gate, at Tirzah, the child died. Jeroboam reigned twenty-two years; but little is said of
his latter years ; we only read that he warred, and that
he reigned. These matters may appear important in
the day when they happen, but in a few years the remembrance of such events is gone by.

ASA.

REIGNED FORTY-ONE YEARS.

[B. C. 970—929.]

Asa succeeded his father Abijah in the government of
the kingdom of Judah ; his reign was long and prosperous, which is thus accounted for—" He did that
which was good and right in the eyes of the Lord his
God ;" " His heart was perfect with the Lord all his
days." He was sincerely devoted to the Lord ; and
where there are good principles in the heart, there will
be good fruit in the life. Accordingly, he put a stop
to the abominations which had been introduced into
Judah, and destroyed the idols. The kingdom was
quiet, and he availed himself of this to fortify several
cities of his dominions, expressly acknowledging that
the rest they enjoyed was of the Lord, because they
had sought him, and therefore they looked for his

blessing on the means used. The result is stated : " so they built, and prospered ;" and we know that .

Except the Lord, with arm Divine,
The pillar'd dome susta:n,
No more the gold and marble shine,
But ruin loads the plain.

The effect of this reformation plainly appeared—the land continued in peace ten years ; after which, Zerah, the Ethiopian, invaded Judah with a very numerous army, but Asa was supported by his subjects, and before the battle joined he offered up a short but most earnest prayer, " Lord, it is nothing with thee to help, whether with many, or with them that have no power : help us, O Lord our God ; for we rest on thee, and in thy name we go against this multitude." This is the genuine language of true faith, and such faith will always prevail. The Ethiopians were wholly defeated at Mareshah, and great spoil fell into the hands of the victors ; but there were other results from this battle.

Azariah the prophet went out to meet Asa, under the direct influence of the Holy Spirit, and addressed the conquerors, " Hear ye me, Asa, and all Judah and Benjamin : The Lord is with you, while ye be with him ; and if ye seek him, he will be found of you ; but if ye forsake him, he will forsake you." He then described the awful and distressed state of Israel, and urged the king and the people of Judah to be confirmed in the true faith, and to root out idolatry. This address had the desired effect ; idolatry was rooted out of Judah, and many flocked to Asa from the land of Israel, " when they saw that the Lord his God was with him."

How different the state of Israel at this period ! Nadab, the son of Jeroboam, succeeded his father in the second year of Asa ; very little is recorded. concerning him. He was a wicked prince, and his reign was short. He had not reigned two years when Baasha, probably one of his officers, slew him while engaged in the siege of Gibbethon, a city of the

H

Philistines, and reigned in his stead. Thus the government of the family of Jeroboam was ended, agreeably
to the Divine threatening.   We shall find, through the
whole history of Judah and Israel, that although the
kingdom of David was divided, yet the Lord Jehovah
continued to exercise the same direct providential interference with both branches of the Jewish people as
in former times.   Prophets were sent, who, in succession, declared to rulers and to subjects, their duties,
warning them of punishment for disobedience ; calamities were sent to check their advance in evil
ways, and removed to encourage them in following
that which was good.   The Jewish government was
still in effect a Theocracy, though the kings ruled much
like those of other nations.   How awful the view thus
given of the depravity and corruption of Israel, under
such a long-continued series of Divine interpositions in
their favour ! and how affecting the expostulations so
frequently expressed by the prophets and psalmist !

" Oh that my people had hearkened unto me,
And Israel had walked in my ways !
I should soon have subdued their enemies,
And turned my hand against their adversaries.
The haters of the Lord should have submitted themselves unto him :
But their time should have endured for ever." Psa. lxxxi. 13—15.

In the fifteenth year of Asa's reign, a solemn assembly was held at Jerusalem, in the third month, the season of the feast of Pentecost. Seven hundred oxen and
seven thousand sheep were sacrificed, and " they entered into a covenant to seek the Lord God of their
fathers with all their heart and soul."   It was a solemn
national covenant, the vast multitude declaring their
assent, outwardly at least, with grateful hearts and joyful lips, and with the solemn sound of instruments used
in the sacred services of the temple.   The people rejoiced, because they had " sought the Lord with their
whole desire ;" and wherever this is done, whether by
nations, families, or individuals, he will be found of
them, At this time, if not earlier, Asa removed his

grandmother from the dignity and authority she possessed as queen-mother, because she had made an idol in a grove—had set up some vile image, and surrounded it with the shady obscurity of a grove, that abominable rites might be practised in secret. Asa's reformation, however, was imperfect, for he allowed the high places to remain, the lofty buildings on elevated spots where idolatrous rites had been practised. But the temple services were again resumed, with as full an approach to their original splendour as the altered circumstances of the nation permitted.

The national covenant was followed by a considerable interval of rest, and presented a very decided contrast to the distracted state of Israel, where Baasha followed up the murder of Nadab by the slaughter of all the descendants of Jeroboam. He left not any that breathed. Thus the denunciation against that prince was fulfilled. Baasha began with a wicked act, and continued in a wicked course. A prophet, Jehu the son of Hanani, was sent to remind him to whom he owed his exaltation, and to denounce the Divine judgments, because he had made Israel to sin. Such a character could not be on friendly terms with Asa, but we do not find any decided effort against him, till the twenty-fifth year of Asa's reign, when he invaded Judah, and seizing Ramah, a strong place to the north of Jerusalem, he began to fortify it as a post from whence he might distress Asa and his subjects, and check the resort of Israel to Judah. The course pursued on this occasion by the king of Judah was wrong, and we cannot account for it. Whether it arose from a desire to avoid direct collision between two divisions of the same people does not appear, but he purchased the assistance of Benhadad, king of Syria, and induced him to invade the northern districts of Israel. This interference caused Baasha to abandon his works at Ramah ; and Asa, assembling the people of Judah, demolished what had been erected, and having removed the materials, used them to strengthen other places.

This act of Asa was the beginning of that system of calling in the aid of neighbouring nations, which ended in the destruction of Israel and Judah. It was rejecting the Divine aid, and seeking help from man instead of God. Hanani, the prophet, was sent to rebuke the king; he reminded him of his great deliverance from the Ethiopians, and told him that the consequences of his sinful, foolish conduct, would be, that thenceforth he should have wars. The words of the prophet are very important: "The eyes of the Lord run to and fro throughout the whole earth, to show himself strong in the behalf of them whose heart is perfect towards him." This counsel should be deeply imprinted on the hearts of all, whether rulers or subjects. But Asa, instead of attending to the warning he received, showed himself forgetful of the Lord; he was wroth with the seer, and put him in prison. This excited a considerable sensation in Judah, but Asa persisted in his wrong course, and silenced the faithful remonstrances of his subjects by oppressive actions.

The death of Baasha, in the following year, prevented farther hostilities against Judah, and we now proceed to notice the rapid changes in the government of Israel which followed. Elah, the son of Baasha, reigned a short two years. His end was awful; a dissolute prince, he was drinking himself drunk at Tirzah, in the house of his steward, when Zimri slew him, and reigned in his stead; and, following the cruel course so general amongst eastern despots, he exterminated the family of his predecessor. But the reign of this murderer was short indeed. The army of Israel was again engaged in the siege of Gibbethon, and on the news of the murder of Elah, they chose their general, Omri, for their king. He marched at once to Tirzah, and forced an entrance into the city, upon which Zimri set fire to the palace, choosing to perish in the flames rather than to fall into the hands of the assailants. But a part of the nation did not approve this military appointment, and chose Tibni for their king; a contest ensued which lasted six years, when it was ended by the death of Tibni, and Omri reigned without a rival. He did worse than all before him : such is the short but comprehensive statement of the inspired historian.

Omri removed the royal residence to a more agreeable and fruitful situation ; he purchased the hill Samaria, and there built the city which was called by that name, making it the royal residence. But he prepared it for others rather than for himself, as he lived only six years after the death of his competitor, when he was succeeded by his son Ahab.

During this miserable state of affairs in Israel, Judah remained in comparative ease, although Asa's character still declined. His sun shone brighter at rising than when setting. In his latter days he was afflicted with a grievous disease in his feet, and having rejected the Divine counsel sent him by the prophet, he farther showed his declension, by seeking "not to the Lord, but to physicians ;" he trusted wholly in the medical art, without imploring the Divine blessing upon the means used. After two years of suffering, he died, and was buried with honourable ceremonies : the people were mindful of his best days. Sin is indeed a down-hill road, and even in the people of God its ill effects and its ill consequences are to be seen, and these things are recorded for our admonition.

Elijah and the widow of Zarephath.—See page 83.

JEHOSHAPHAT.

REIGNED TWENTY-FIVE YEARS.

[B.C. 929—904.]

JEHOSHAPHAT was the son of Asa, whom he succeeded
in the throne of Judah. He prospered, because he
sought the first ways of his father and of David. In
2 Chron. xvii. is an account of the early measures of
his reign. He sought the Lord God of his father : he
was earnest in prayer : he was answered : " his heart
was lifted up in the ways of the Lord." Prayer for
the Divine guidance never will be offered in vain ; and,
being thus " lifted up," he was enabled to overcome
the difficulties in his way, even those things which
had been hinderances to his father Asa ; he took
away the high places and groves out of Judah. Well
is it for us when we, in every station and calling, seek
to be " lifted up" by Him who has promised to support

his people. Jehoshaphat fortified the cities of Judah, and those in a part of Ephraim, which his father had succeeded in occupying. The Lord inclined the hearts of the people to support his government, and he sent princes, and priests, and Levites, through his land, to instruct his subjects ; they had the book of the law of the Lord with them, they were lecturers, preaching ministers ; they made the Scriptures known to the people. Trouble must be expected both by kings and princes, if they take no care that the people should be taught in the law of the Lord ; no instruction will avail where that is not the foundation.

" When a man's ways please the Lord, he maketh even his enemies to be at peace with him." We read that " the fear of the Lord fell upon all the kingdoms of the lands that were round about Judah, so that they made no war against Jehoshaphat." Not only his own people, but the Philistines and Arabians also, willingly brought him presents and tribute. The offerings of the latter were characteristic of the pastoral habits of the people, large flocks of sheep and goats. He had much business in the cities of Judah ; outward blessings were especially promised to those who kept the Divine covenant under the Old Testament dispensation, and even now, attention to the ways of peace and godliness will often promote our worldly, as it always does our spiritual interests. Jehoshaphat had a well-organized military arrangement, ready for action ; but though well prepared to meet an enemy, we do not find that he thought of conquests.

We must now return to Israel, which will claim a considerable portion of our attention. That unhappy kingdom had a respite from the civil dissensions and mutual slaughter by which it lately suffered so severely ; but in other respects it presented a painful contrast to the state of Judah. Its king was Ahab, and under him bad became still worse. " He did evil in the sight of the Lord above all that were before him." He sinned more openly than his predecessors ;

for he took to wife Jezebel, the daughter of Ethbaal,
king of the Zidonians : she is connected with general
history, being the aunt of Dido, the foundress of Car-
thage. By her beauty and address she obtained a
commanding and fatal influence over the king of
Israel, similar to what has been exemplified in various
instances of European history. Under the ascendancy
of this fascinating, but imperious and wicked female,
Ahab's easy temper was led onward in evil ways ; he
threw off the worship of Jehovah, even in the mutilated and more than half idolatrous state, according to
which it had been conducted under the forms devised
by Jeroboam. The king served Baal, and built a
temple for that vile heathen deity at Samaria. He
made a grove for the abominations of the secret idolatrous worship, and " did more to provoke the Lord
God of Israel to anger than all the kings of Israel
that were before him." The worship of Jehovah was
utterly suppressed, and only one individual remained
who dared openly to stand forth as a follower of the
true God. Yet this state of darkness was not brought
over the land without a struggle. A number of prophets testified against it, though the priests and Levites had long since been driven from the land of
Israel. Persecution was called forth, and Jezebel
caused these prophets to be cut off ; they were put to
death without remorse, except a hundred of them,
who were concealed in two of the intricate caverns of
the land, in which they were protected and fed by the
kind care of Obadiah, one of Ahab's ministers, whom
God strengthened to remain faithful, even in the
wicked and persecuting court to which he belonged.

And now, amidst this dark and gloomy scene, a
brilliant light from above bursts upon our view, in the
character and actions of the prophet Elijah, whose
history and acts are recorded as instructions for the
ministers of the Lord, when called to rebuke a sinful
generation. " Then," to use the words of the writer
of the book of Ecclesiasticus, " stood up Elias the pro-

phet as fire, and his word burned like a lamp." It was lighted with fire from heaven. His history and that of Joseph stand forth more prominently than any others recorded in the Old Testament. The reader should now lay aside this book, and read carefully the deeply interesting particulars recorded in the Bible, from the seventeenth chapter of the First Book of Kings to the second chapter of the Second Book. To transcribe these chapters is needless, to attempt to supply a complete narrative in other words, is worse than unnecessary. We will suppose the Scripture narrative is read, and impressed upon the reader's memory, and will only notice the leading features. To go fully and properly into the details, would fill a much larger space than can' be allotted to the whole of this work : it is not intended for a history of Elijah, but of the kings of Judah and Israel.

When darkness had covered the land, and gross darkness the people, when the hills smoked with sacrifices to Baal and Ashtaroth, and the groves witnessed the licentious rites of idol worship, and both hills and groves resounded with the yells of the priests of false gods, and the wild music used in their observances ; while the king was presiding at these orgies, or consulting what steps should be taken to extend and enforce this system, an unknown man suddenly appeared in the royal presence. Of plain but commanding aspect, clad with a rough and hairy mantle, he confronts the idolatrous monarch, and delivers a short but emphatic message. " As Jehovah the God of Israel liveth, before whom I stand, there shall not be dew nor rain these years, but according to my word." He turned and departed. His manner and tone commanded respect ; for the moment he was unmolested, and when Ahab was stirred up to order the stranger to be secured, he had gone forth no one knew whither. A search was ordered, but by the Divine direction he had proceeded to the banks of the Jordan. There, in a solitary spot, amid rocky cliffs, winding cavities, and tangled thickets, the prophet found a secure retreat. But how shall he be fed? The Lord who sent him thither will provide : duly at morn and eve the ravens, whose nests are built in the crag beneath which he reposes, bring him supplies of bread and flesh. Not the carrion prey they seek for their young, but guided by miraculous impulse, though of themselves more likely to rob than to feed, they wing their way to some spot where provision suited for human sustenance is found, they bring it and place it at the prophet's feet. The course of nature shall be changed sooner than one of God's promises shall fail. Down this narrow and tangled vale a brook glided towards Jordan and supplied the prophet's thirst. Here he sat communing with his God ; day after day passed, but he waited patiently till directed by the Lord to remove. Self-examination, prayer, and converse with his God, will always furnish employment for the believer.

Meanwhile the clouds dropped not rain at the accustomed period ; the heavy dews usual in that country fail.

No rain-drops fall, no dew-fraught cloud at morn,
Or closing eve, creeps slowly up the vale ;
The withering herbage dies ; among the palms,
The shrivell'd leaves send to the summer gale
An autumn rustle ; no sweet songster's lay
Is warbled from the branches ; scarce is heard
The rill's faint brawl. The prophet looks around,
And trusts in God, and lays his doomed head
Upon the flowerless bank ; serene he sleeps,
Nor wakes till dawning.

The general appearance of the sun-scorched plains of Palestine is dry and barren during the summer months, but now autumn and winter succeed without the accustomed copious rains, and the scanty supplies of moisture hardly suffice to keep expiring nature from utter desolation. The torrent brook daily wastes. The prophet beholds it with thoughts of doubt, but the ravens still wing their way with daily food, and though the water seems about to fail, his faith fails not, he knows that the Lord will provide. Nor will the faith of any believer be disappointed. When the brook was dried, but not till then, the prophet was directed to go to Zarephath. Happy is the believer who can thus calmly wait the Divine direction, not in indolence, but in faith, knowing that all his times are in the hand of the Lord—all events at his command.

" My times are in Thy hand,"
  My God, I wish them there ;
My life, my friends, my soul I leave,
  Entirely to thy care.

" My times are in Thy hand,"
  Whatever they may be,
Pleasing or painful, dark or bright,
  As best may seem to Thee.

" My times are in Thy hand,"
  Why should I doubt or fear ?
My Father's hand will never cause
  His child a needless tear.

The prophet was farther informed that a widow in the city of Zarephath was appointed or commanded to sustain him. There were thousands of widows in Israel and Judah at that time, but to none of them was the prophet sent ; and he hesitated not to go according to the Divine command, although it was a weary way, through a parched and withered country. The place to which he was ordered to proceed, was the native land of the wretched persecuting idolatress, at whose instigation Ahab was making the strictest search for the prophet, yet he went forward in safety and assurance, and at last he beheld the smoke of the " city of furnaces." Hungry and faint he drew near the gate, and there he saw a widow preparing a scanty meal for her child and herself ; the underwood was abundant and withered, and fuel needed not to be collected till the time for using it arrived. That errand brought her forth at the very time when Divine Providence guided Elijah to the entrance of her city. Evidently she was poor ; the last expected meal was scanty, two sticks would suffice to bake

the handful of flour; but if God appointed her to
sustain Elijah, means would not be wanting.   Her reply showed inability, but it also showed that she re-
verenced him as a prophet, a follower of Jehovah,
although her soul must have been engrossed with
bitter thoughts, for she was occupied in preparing
what she had reason to apprehend would be the last
meal for herself and a beloved child!   What induced
her to show this respect to Elijah?   Surely we need
not stop to inquire, knowing that her heart was under
the direction of Him who had caused ravens to minister to his servant.   Months had gone by since Elijah
had conversed with one who gave utterance to the
name of his Lord, and he hesitated not to speak to
the destitute, anxious widow, with all the confidence
of faith.   She was enabled to show the like faith ;
she delayed not to put her hand into her barrel or
earthern jar, to draw forth the last handful of meal ;
she hesitated not to pour the last drop of oil from her
cruse, and thus she supplied the prophet's need.   But
she also found the words of the prophet fulfilled.   The
handful of meal still remained undiminished, the cruse
still supplied oil, and she and her fa ily drew sustenance from that barrel and that cruse for a full year.
With what lively faith must they have communed, as
the days rolled away, and each day brought a miraculous supply, while the busy traders, among whom they
dwelt, wasted not a thought upon the lonely widow,
and the obscure Israelite, her guest, or else regarded
them with scorn!   Surely the christian believer at the
present day is as much indebted to the special Providence of God for daily mercies, as Elijah and the
widow of Zarephath.   But we do not feel the same
lively faith, and the same gush of thankfulness towards
our Lord, when we draw from a well-supplied store, as
when we go day by day expecting that the last crust
is consumed, and yet find another graciously imparted
to our need.   Nor is this remark to be confined to
supplies of food.   There are daily mercies needed by

persons of every rank, and for these they are as de-
pendent as the beggar for his daily bread.

A still harder trial of faith was sent, the child died
—the mother reproached the prophet. He uttered no
angry reply, but demanded her son. Her faith failed
not, she gave the body to the prophet. The special
prayer of Elijah was heard, the child was restored.

> ——————The prophet raised
> The renovated child; and on that breast
> Which gave the life-stream of its infancy,
> Laid the fair head once more.—If ye would know
> Aught of that 'wildering trance of ecstacy,
> Go to a mother's heart, but question not
> So poor a thing as language.

The prayer of such faith as that of Elijah assuredly
shall be granted. Christian professor, Elijah was a
man of like passions with thee : art thou of like faith
with the prophet? or even of the widow of Zarephath ;
canst thou surrender even a dead child, some blighted
desire of thy bosom, to one whom thou believest to be
a messenger of God? And art not thou ready to
think the minister of the Lord a messenger of ill to
thee, when his words or his deeds cause thy sins to
come to thy remembrance ?

Another year was past, and the famine was sore in
the land.

> There fell no rain in Israel : the sad trees
> Reft of their coronals, and the crisp'd vines
> And flowers whose dewless bosoms sought the dust,
> Mourn'd the long drought. The miserable herds
> Pin'd on, and perish'd 'mid the scorching fields.
> And near the vanish'd fountains where they us'd
> Freely to slake their thirst, the mourning flocks
> Laid their parch'd mouths and died.

The splendid palace richly adorned with ivory,
erected by Ahab in the fertile valley of Jezreel, no
longer commanded a prospect over a verdant and
pleasing tract. All was one uniformly brown, withered,
and parched scene. And the king now was anxious
for the few that remained of his wasted cattle. This
brings before us another servant of Jehovah, in a place

I

still less likely for him to be found than in the city of
Zarephath. One of Ahab's chief ministers feared the
Lord, he feared Him greatly, and had feared him from
his early youth; but with the fear to disoblige a kind
father, not with the servile fear of an unwilling slave.
And nothing but especial grace, deeply impressed on
his soul, could have kept him thus, a decided believer,
in the house of Ahab! Why had he continued there?
It was a post of duty; he had been enabled by his
power and station to rescue and support the persecuted
ministers of Jehovah. Then let us not shrink from the
difficulty of any station to which we are lawfully called,
or where God places us; let us not fail to fulfil its
duties, and he will guide and support us there.

While the king and his minister were on their way
through the land, to look for some remaining patches of
verdure, an employment frequent in the east during
long-continued droughts, Elijah received a command,
exercising his faith even more than those which pre-
ceded. "Go, show thyself to Ahab, and I will send
rain upon the earth." He hesitated not, but went.
Obadiah met the prophet, and was startled at his direction to tell the king that Elijah was there. He
doubted not but that the Lord would preserve the prophet, but he feared lest he should himself be exposed
to danger; yet, on receiving the prophet's assurance,
he went to seek Ahab.

The haughty tyrant tried to shake Elijah, by reproaching him as the troubler of Israel, but his lion
spirit quailed not. He at once referred the troubles of
the land to their true source, the iniquity of its rulers.
Elijah instructed the king to assemble the people and
the idolatrous prophets, at mount Carmel. The king
obeyed. How clear an illustration of the words of
Solomon, "The king's heart is in the hand of the
Lord, as the rivers of water; he turneth it whitherso-
ever he will." Ahab obeyed the desire of Elijah, and
that without delay. And, as in the case of Daniel, the
Lord shut the mouth of the lion.

Carmel is a rocky mass rising abruptly from the sea, for the most part covered with scanty verdure, and only a few cedars and inferior shrubs grace its ascent; but in the days of the kings it was fruitful, and richly wooded, and even now, in the glad season of spring, the rich variety of flowering heaths, and other wild blossoms with which its heights are covered, recall to mind the expressions of the prophets, when they speak of the richly decked head of Carmel. And still the same prospect, as in the days of Elijah, stretches on either hand; to the west, the Mediterranean Sea, with its blue waters and the white sails flitting along its bosom; to the east, the view extends over the fertile plain of Esdraelon, with mount Tabor rising abruptly in the distance; on the north is seen the storm-clad tops of giant Lebanon, with all the variety of its lower elevation; immediately beneath is that ancient river, the river Kishon, and the eye wanders over many a spot once noted in the history of Israel.

But though the nation was depressed at the time of which we speak, how much more depressed now! At the time under consideration, Elijah stood on this height, appearing alone as a prophet of the Lord, opposed to four hundred and fifty idolatrous prophets, and a multitude whose minds were hesitating between two opinions. They had not entirely forgotten the mighty works of Jehovah, but they preferred the worldly enjoyments and pleasures promoted by idolatry. Alas, that so many among us "halt between two opinions," and are willing to declare their belief in the Lord Jehovah, or in the idol Baal, as they consider their interest to be!

Elijah shrunk not from the arduous trial. The results should be read in the words of Scripture, 1 Kings xviii. There the reader will mark the selection of the victim and the preparations for the sacrifice by the idolatrous priests, who called on their god from morning till noon; but no response could be obtained from a fabled being; and the open situation, devoid of those masses of foliage which usually sheltered their deceptions and crimes,

under the steady gaze of the surrounding multitude, left
no opportunity for fraudulent trickery. They exhibited their frantic gesticulations, but the prophet, with
deep-toned irony, derided their vain attempts, reminding them of the heathen ideas of deity, which supposed
their god a being of like passions with themselves.
" He is talking, or rather he is meditating ; he is pursuing, engaged in the chase ; he is in a journey; per-
adventure he sleepeth, and must be awakened :   Cry
aloud then, to gain his attention ! " All this is applicable to the letter, at the present day, in reference to the
heathen deities of the east and their votaries, who believe the gods to be thus occupied, and thus seek to
rouse their attention !   But self-inflicted pains, extra-
vagant actions, and frantic cries were alike in vain.
The created object which they adored shone in burning splendour, but even its meridian rays kindled not
the desired flame.   And now the hour for the evening
sacrifice was come, Elijah repaired a ruined altar
formerly used in the service of Jehovah ; he placed
the wood and the victim in the accustomed form, and
after drenching the pile with repeated effusions of water, he offered up a prayer at once affecting and sublime.   A solemn pause ensued—what varying expressions must have appeared in the countenances of
the assembled multitude ! not one could stand in apa-
thy and indifference.   The prayer of Elijah was heard.
Fire from heaven fell upon the spot—the victim, the
wood, the water, the dust around, all disappeared in
the sacred flame, while even the stones of the altar
testified the reality of its intensely consuming power.
An answer so unquestionable convinced the people,
and they exclaimed, " Jehovah, he is God." Are
proofs of this wanting at the present day ?   Assuredly
not ; yet the god of our politicians, of our philosophers,
of our men of business, and our men of fashion, is not
Jehovah ; and though there is a being of their own
fancy, upon whom they call in the hour of difficulty
and distress, there is for them neither voice, nor any to

answer, nor any that regardeth; this is manifested
every day, but still they will not choose the Lord for
their God!

The dispensation under which Israel then lived,
made idol-worship treason against the Most High.
The prophets of Baal and Ashtaroth were therefore worthy of death. At the Divine command, as
signified by Elijah, they were seized, and their blood
crimsoned the scanty stream of the river Kishon; we
may be thankful that we live under a different dispensation, and that we are not required thus to execute
the Divine judgments. These judgments, however,
are not less sure; unbelievers may escape in this life,
but they will suffer in that which is to come.

Ahab's conduct showed that he was subject to the
Power that can influence the heart. He objected not
to the execution of Jezebel's wicked favourites, and
when Elijah told him to dismiss his cares, for rain was
at hand, he seems to have believed the promise of the
blessing. The prophet ascended the highest cliff of
Carmel, and directed his servant to look toward the
sea, while he assumed the eastern posture of deep
thought and earnest supplication. Prayer was as meat
and drink to Elijah; he knew that it was not so to
Ahab, and he told the king to gratify his appetite,
while he wrestled with the Lord in prayer, and watched
for an answer. Six times the servant looked out, over
the face of the deep, and returned the same reply,
" There is nothing." But this only made Elijah more
earnest in prayer—

> And though the blazing sun had spread
> A sky of brass above his head,
> Though the parch'd earth through years nor knew
> The gracious rain, nor gentle dew;
> Strong in the promise and the power,
> Faith's ear drank in the coming shower,
> And still with prayer, he waits the hour.

At last he was told that a small cloud, like a man's
hand, had appeared. He then saw the promise already opening to fulfilment, and hastened the king's

I 2

return homeward, before the torrents, streaming from the heights, should impede his way. He declared, "There is a sound of abundance of rain;" and, with more than natural strength, ran before the royal chariot, unchecked by the storm and tempest, till he entered the palace of Jezreel. Let us not forget, that an inspired apostle refers to this narrative as an encouragement to perseverance in supplication; but every book of Scripture produces instances of the achievements of prayer, though not always accompanied by circumstances which so forcibly impress the mind: and it is the spirit in which the plea is offered, not the form or circumstances of the request, that avail. It still is a yearly-custom, on the supposed anniversary of Elijah's sacrifice, for homage to be paid to Elijah on this spot, and at a pile which may contain some of the very stones he gathered for this occasion. But how different the spirit of the mohammedans, or nominal christians, who assemble on this occasion, and what indignant expressions would burst from the lips of the prophet, were he sent to earth again to stand in the multitude assembled on mount Carmel!

Elijah now was in the royal city. Perhaps he expected that the miraculous interference just displayed, would have resulted in the return of Israel, both king and people, to Jehovah. There is no reason to suppose that he desired great things for himself, but it is evident that he thought he knew what would be most for the glory of the Lord; and that the Lord, who seeth not as man seeth, had other views than those of the prophet, and that Elijah was about to be disappointed.

Jezebel had witnessed the war of elements, she saw the earth refreshed, famine stayed, and her subjects saved from perishing, but her prophets were no more! The ministers of superstition and of pleasure were gone! She therefore determined on the death of Elijah; but, in the storm of her passions, she warned him of his danger. The prophet was startled at this mes-

sage ; the dream in which it is probable he was indulging dispersed, his faith failed !　He forgot that the fire
from heaven, which consumed his sacrifice, could be
sent to protect his person, and to destroy his enemies.

Elijah arose and went for his life.　Without wait-
ing for the Divine direction, perhaps without asking
specially for it, he hastened through Samaria and Judea, and leaving his servant at the last cluster of human habitations, he pressed forward a day's journey
into the solitary wilderness.　At evening he sunk down

oeneath a stunted shrub, weary of his painful conflicts,
and, as he thought, fruitless labours.　How strong a
lesson to the believer not to be weary in well doing,
and to beware not to attempt to stand in his own
strength.　Beware of murmuring and discontent.　Hear
the complaining prophet, " It is enough ; now, O
Lord, take away my life, for I am not better than my
fathers."　The request was hasty, the complaint showed
want of faith ; but might it not in some degree proceed
from the disappointment of his hopes ?　He had lately

stood honoured in the sight of all Israel ; pride is a sub-
tle enemy, and creeps into the bosom of the most distinguished saint ; and it is, well for every one who is
called to stand forth as the servant of the Lord, that he
should be reminded, " he is not better than his fathers."
It is well for him, that his favourite schemes, those
which he has revolved through many a day and many
a night, fully believing that his employment in them
would tend to the glory of his Master, should be suffered to slip from his grasp, or that he should even be
forced to resign them, and be taught that the purposes of the Lord shall stand, though his expectations,
cherished perhaps through many years, are spoiled,
like the tender grapes upon the vines by the foxes,
or are scattered like the sands of the desert before the
whirlwind.

The Lord will not forget his people, though their
faith may for a time be clouded by carnal doubts and
unbecoming fears ; and though a christian will have to
suffer if he rushes unbidden into a wilderness, yet still
the Lord may meet him there in mercy.   Death was
not sent to Elijah, but a refreshing sleep.   Bread and
water were supplied to the weary traveller ; he fed on
this miraculous food, and was refreshed ; he was directed as to his onward course, and went forward with
renewed vigour.   Thus the believer is taught to dismiss corroding cares ; bread is not only sent to the
servant of God in this wilderness, but it is prepared for
him while he is sleeping, when the Lord sees fit ;
though it is best for us that we, for the most part, have
to prepare it for ourselves.

Elijah continued his course with unabated ardour,
across the sandy plains and over the rocky heights
of the desert.   It was that desert, " the waste howling
wilderness," through which the tribes of Israel had
been led by the pillar of cloud and of fire.   The history of olden time would arise in his mind, and support his spirits under the lonely way, till the dark

masses of Horeb rose in the distance. This was a
solace to his weary limbs, declaring his approach to
the spot where Israel had communed with their God.
At length Elijah found himself at the foot of the rocky
mountain, whose height had for some time towered in
the distance, and then had been lost to his view as he
descended the interposing valleys. It was Horeb, the
mount of God; nor was it difficult to find a cave
amidst its rocky precipices, to afford a shelter from
the heat by day and the cold by night. His mind appears yet to have been in an uncertain state; from
this he is roused by the abrupt and startling inquiry,
"What doest thou here, Elijah?" Would that this
question was sounded with the same force and energy
in the ears of every secure sinner and careless professor. The prophet replied, urging his zeal for the
Lord, and complaining that all his efforts seemed to be
fruitless. His mind was not in a right state; he
seemed ready to expostulate with his God, and still to
repine that his own plans were overruled. He was directed to leave the dark cavern, and to stand upon the
mount before the Lord. Let the believer, when op-
pressed and worn down, go forth in spirit from the
dark cavern of his own heart, and behold the wonders
of redeeming love. Let him stand upon the mount
before the Lord. Even the frowning summits of Horeb, the dread depository of the law, are a more profitable sight than the vile imagery of our own hearts,
and our deadness and depravity; but how blessed the
view of Calvary, the glimpse of a Saviour's love.

Let us picture to our minds the spot where the prophet then stood. The vast and gloomy precipices;
the granite mountains piled on each other, and all the
wild sublimity of that scene, with its historical recollections. Imagine a most terrific tempest, rending the
tops of the rugged rocks, and an earthquake upheav-
ing their firmly-seated base, while sheets of fire involve the heights around. The prophet stands unhurt

amidst this more than elemental conflict, and meditates
upon the power of the Most High.   He feels that he is
a mere worm, the insect of a day, before the Almighty,
Him that sitteth upon the circle of the earth, in whose
hand Horeb and Sinai are but as the dust of the ba-
lance, who taketh up the isles as a very little thing,
who even stretcheth out the heavens as a curtain, and
spreadeth them out as a tent to dwell in.   The tempest, the earthquake, the fire, successively pass away ;
still the prophet's mind realizes no sense of the Divine
presence.   The world may be hurled into ruin, and
yet no peaceful sense of God's favour be vouchsafed.
Often do we behold this in the disappointed hopes
and dreadful catastrophes of hardened impenitent sinners.   But now, all is hushed and in repose.   The
masses so lately agitated and conflicting with each
other, seem as though they had never been moved.
A still small voice is heard.   The prophet wonders
and adores ; he owns his present Lord.   His heart is
touched with a sense of tender mercy ; he feels that
though but a feeble worm, yet he is not forgotten by
the Almighty Ruler of nature.   He feels that the
thunders of the law are less powerful than the still,
gentle voice of the gospel.   And, reader, was it never
so with you ?   Even if the gentle whispers of the gospel have not been heard, has not the small still voice
of conscience penetrated deeper into your heart than
the outward dispensations of Divine Providence ?
Have you never heard in the mart of traffic, in the
haunts of pleasure, in the gay delusive scenes of the
one, and amid the soul-engrossing commerce of the
other, have *you* never heard the still small voice within
your breast, asking with pointed accents, " What doest
thou here ?"   Let the young who read these pages
learn never to scorn this silent monitor, nor attempt to
check the warning ; and reader, if you have not heard
it in former days, listen ! Do you not hear it *now ?*   It
is the voice of your heavenly Father !

Speak, gracious Lord, speak ever thus,
  And let thy terrors prove
The harbingers of peace to us,
  The heralds of thy love !
Come through the earthquake, fire, and storm,
Come in the mildest, sweetest form,
  And all our fears remove ;
One word from Thee is all we claim—
Be that one word, a Saviour's name!

The inquiry is again renewed, " What doest thou
here, Elijah ?" The message of the law and of the
gospel, although they strike differently upon the outward senses, equally direct us to consider our state, and
how we can stand in the Divine presence. The prophet's answer is the same as before, but now it seems
rather the expression of an assured faith than the dic-
tates of an unbelieving spirit. This appears the more
probable, from the simple acquiescence with which Elijah received his renewed commission, and went forth to
execute it. He is to appoint Hazael to be king over
Syria, Jehu to be king of Israel, and Elisha to be his
own successor ; but it is remarkable that Jehu was not
to be anointed by Elijah, nor by Elisha, but by a young
man long afterwards. Here is an answer to each of
the clauses of his complaint. Has Israel forsaken the
covenant ? Hazael is to be appointed the rod of God's
anger. Has Israel, under Ahab, thrown down the altars of Jehovah, and slain the prophets of the Lord ?
Jehu is to be called forth, to exterminate the wicked
rulers at whose bidding these acts were done. Is Elijah left alone, and his life endangered ? Elisha shall
be qualified to go forth as his successor. Thus the
gloomy apprehensions of the prophet are done away ;
he sees that the Lord has a cure for every evil. Nay
more, he is assured that there are yet seven thousand
in Israel, who have not bowed to Baal. How wrong
is our estimate as to the church of God ! how apt are
we to form our judgment from the limited scope within
our view, instead of simply relying on the assurances
of God's word ! We doubt as to the existence of
things plainly declared in the word of God, because we

do not see them. " I, I only am left!" What a
statement to proceed from the lips of a poor short-
sighted mortal, respecting the declarations of an all-
seeing God! We see not the stars in the day-time,
yet they are fixed in the firmament, and when the
evening shades prevail, when the glare which now af-
fects our sight is removed, they will be plainly dis-
cerned. The saints of the Most High may not be seen
while the scorching sunbeams of persecution prevail,
but they are visible when that consuming heat has
passed. And, reader, have *you* been "jealous for the
Lord?" Do you seek after idols, or do you abhor the
dreams of ambition, the enticements of gain, and the
allurements of pleasure? What is your occupation,
what is the tenor of your pursuits in this world; do you
expect in the last, the great and solemn day, that it
shall be said to you, " Thou hast done well here?"

The prophet left the desert, a wiser and a better man
than when he first trod its mazes. He sought the valley of the Jordan; there, in the fruitful plains near the
town of Abel-meholah, he found the son and the servants of Shaphat, availing themselves of the late favourable change. The ground softened by the rain,
now yielded to the ploughshare, and efforts were made
to regain part of the time that had been lost. A traveller drew near. It was the prophet whose fame had resounded through the land, Elijah the Tishbite. He
passed Elisha, and threw his mantle upon the shoulders
of the unpretending youth. Elisha understood the call,
and hastened after the prophet. He stood not to consider the worldly advantages he was to relinquish, or
how his temper and abilities fitted him for the office.
The call was clear, and where it is so, every needful
gift will be bestowed. He ran after the prophet, only
requesting leave to bid farewell to his beloved parents.
Elijah consented; this was not a case in which the parental feelings would be opposed to the Divine summons.
Elisha bade farewell to his family, and this by a feast
upon a sacrifice; not offered with the ritual and cere-

monial observances of the temple worship, but a family
service, offered in simple faith, and as such, accepted of
the Lord. Elisha then arose and followed Elijah, and
ministered unto him. Reader, if the Lord your God gives
you a clear summons to his service, are you ready to
take leave of your friends, to sacrifice worldly prospects, and to use the instruments of your worldly profession in making this sacrifice more complete, and to
give up willingly to others the worldly advantages you
might yourself have possessed? All this will readily
be done, under the influence of God the Holy Spirit,
if he cause but a corner or a shred of the prophetic mantle to touch you.

The idolatries of Israel's princes had weakened the
land, and exposed it to the attacks of its enemies.
Benhadad, the king of Syria, besieged Samaria with a
powerful force. Ahab consented to become tributary
to him, but refused the farther demand, to submit to
general plunder and spoliation. To the boasting threat
of the Syrian king, Ahab gave a short reply, on
many occasions it may be appositely applied—" Let not
him that girdeth on his harness boast like him that
taketh it off." Boast not at the beginning of any affair.
Benhadad received this answer when engaged in a
drunken carouse, and ordered an immediate attack on
Samaria. Ahab was encouraged by the word of a prophet, for God had not yet turned his mercy from Israel; and the Syrians were defeated—the first onset of
the Israelites being successfully made by the servants
of the chiefs, and not by the regularly disciplined troops.
In the following year the land was again invaded, and
the Syrians resolved to fight on the plains, deeming
the God of Israel to be a Deity whose power was confined to the hills. Pagan idolatry always peoples the
various objects of nature with different, and often with
discordant deities. The heathen " find gods in every
thing," but how widely different from the Almighty
Omnipresent Jehovah. The Lord will vindicate his
honour; the Syrians were again defeated, and with

K

great slaughter. Benhadad fled to Aphek, where a
further destruction of his army took place; he concealed himself in a chamber within a chamber : such are
common in eastern houses at the present day. His attendants persuaded him to go forth with signs of the
deepest humiliation—the same have been repeatedly
displayed by captive eastern monarchs, both in ancient
and modern times—and to ask for mercy. The king
of Israel, elated by his success, entered into a treaty
with his enemy, on terms which would display his
power, instead of completely subjugating the enemy of
God's people. The Lord sent a prophet to tell Ahab
of his error ; that it would end in his destruction, and
be most injurious to his people; but Ahab repented
not, though he manifested displeasure. It is thought
that this prophet was Micaiah, and that he was impri-
soned for his faithfulness.

We next have a scene of a private nature, but of no
ordinary description : it involved blasphemy, injustice,
treachery, and murder. Ahab, with all his royal pos-
sessions, was not satisfied. He beheld his own do-
mains refreshed by the recent fertilizing showers, but
forgot that the prospect had lately been a barren and
withered desert, till the Divine bounty spake the word
for the pleasing change. Instead of thankfulness to
the Giver of all good, he coveted a small plot of ground,
the family inheritance of Naboth. He offered to pur-
chase it, but Naboth had not bowed the knee to Baal ;
he was attentive to the injunctions of the Divine law
relative to the inheritances in Canaan, and refused to
sell his share in the promised land for a sum of money,
or even to exchange it for any other spot. Would
that men were generally as content with the lot which
God has assigned them in this life. Ahab was displeased at the refusal, and exhibited his feelings in the
same pettish manner as now is often displayed in the
east. He refused to eat, and rejected all the offered
attentions of his servants. When men are disposed to
listen to temptations, Satan soon finds a suitable agent,

and Ahab had his queen always at hand ready to stir him up to evil. Even in those days some forms of justice must be attended to : she caused an accusation for blasphemy to be brought against Naboth ; false witnesses were suborned, Naboth was condemned by judges who knew him to be innocent, and was put to death with his family. This providence was mysterious ; but it is one of the events which we shall understand hereafter.

Jezebel triumphantly informed Ahab of the result, and he rose up to go to the vineyard of Naboth, and take possession of it as a forfeiture. He knew it was obtained by wrong, yet was willing to seize the advantage. Attended by his officers, the king entered the plot of ground, and while busily planning how it should be laid out to form a pleasure garden, a well-known form met his view. It was Elijah! The conscience of the monarch at once brought forward the crime and its results. Sentence was pronounced. At the name of Naboth, stricken with terror, Ahab exclaims, " Hast thou found me, O mine enemy!" How awful the state of that man, be he a beggar or a prince, by whom the minister of God is considered as an " enemy." An awful doom was denounced against the murderers and their posterity. And now for the first time Ahab showed some symptoms of remorse. That he felt sorrow for his crime we may believe, but it was not repentance to life and salvation ; he trembled, not at the sin, but at the punishment. His repentance was regarded with some favour ; because he humbled himself, the full execution of judgment was delayed till the iniquity of his house should be filled up, yet he was not spared from condign punishment. Ahab soon after came to an untimely end, and, agreeably to the word of the Lord, dogs licked his blood in Samaria, where the crime was committed. His outward reformation procured a delay in the execution of the sentence, but he did not avail himself of the respite ; to the last he followed Baal, and regarded the prophets of the Lord as enemies.

To return to the affairs of Judah : we read that Jehoshaphat had riches and honour in abundance, yet he joined affinity with Ahab. How sad a proof that human nature will not be contented with the most ample supply of the blessings of this life ; something *more* is still craved, and sought for. And, what is worst of all, though there is the strongest proof that every blessing we have received has come to us especially from the hand of God, yet additions are sought by crooked and indirect courses. How painful, and yet how instructive, to see the frequent desire even of the believer to form unlawful connexions with the world. Thus Jehoshaphat thought to strengthen his interests by joining in affinity with Ahab. His son married the daughter of Ahab and Jezebel. The disastrous results we shall soon perceive, in the troubles and bloodshed which emanated from his connexion.

This union took place about the thirteenth year of Jehoshaphat. About seven years afterwards he visited Ahab at Samaria, and was received with attention. The king of Judah was prevailed upon to join Ahab in an expedition against the Syrians for the recovery of Ramoth-gilead, but expressed his desire to seek the Divine direction before they proceeded. At the command of Ahab, the prophets of Baal were collected together ; four hundred of them with one voice assured the confederate kings of victory and success. But Jehoshaphat was not satisfied with the unusual scene presented to him by these men. He inquired for a prophet of Jehovah. The idolatrous Ahab unwillingly consented to the introduction of one, assigning as a reason, that this prophet always spoke of evil to him ! He preferred those who prophesied smooth things, however false and deceitful. But Micaiah was sent for, and with simplicity declared his intention to deliver the Divine message, refusing to be guided by the suggestions of the crafty or deluded messenger. He stood before the thrones of the confederate kings, and a tone of bitter irony, told them, " Go up, and prosper." Ahab saw his drift, and could not avoid calling for a more explicit statement of the truth. In answer, the prophet made a statement, whether of a vision, or as a parable, we need not decide : it warned the king of the near approach of his last hour, and unveiled the treachery or deceit of the band of false prophets then gesticulating before them. His reward was the bread and water of affliction.

Ahab still persisted in his plan, and went forth to battle, but with that blind cunning which characterizes the worldling, he thought to secure his own safety by assuming the appearance of a common soldier, while he cared not to expose his friend and ally to increased danger. The combat was joined, the king of Syria had directed an especial attack against Ahab ; this endangered Jehoshaphat, he cried unto the Lord, who caused the Syrians to turn back. Ahab meanwhile thought himself secure in his disguise, but every shaft flies with Divine guidance, and though a Syrian archer drew his bow at a venture, the unerring bolt pursued its allotted course, and not only found Ahab, but entered at a crevice of his armour, and wounded him mortally. He ordered the driver of his chariot to turn from the army :

> Borne from the danger, still the monarch stood,
> And mark'd the strife, though weltering in his blood ;
> Supported in his chariot, till the sun
> Sunk in the west, its glorious journey done ;
> When Syria's banner caught his parting rays,
> And, proud in conquest, floated on the breeze,
> For victory was theirs—while Israel's bands
> Fled in confusion, like the Lybian sands.
> Ahab, as feebler grew his waning sight,
> Saw the disgraceful, the disastrous flight,
> Then clos'd his rayless eyes in everlasting night.

How foolish to think to escape from the word of an Almighty and Omniscient God. Such was the death of Ahab, and according to the word of the Lord, spoken by Elijah, the dogs licked his blood. One other event during his reign is mentioned, the rebuilding of Jericho. It brought upon the builder the curse denounced against any one who should rebuild that devoted city, Josh. vi. 26 ; but when rebuilt, the curse passed away, it had not been denounced against dwellers there.

Jehoshaphat returned home, and was reproved by the prophet Jehu, for " helping the ungodly, and loving those that hate the Lord." Wiser than his father, he profited by the rebuke, and, instead of resenting it, followed the counsel of the psalmist.

" Let the righteous smite me—it shall be a kindness:
And let him reprove me—it shall be an excellent oil, which shall not
        break my head :
For yet my prayer also shall be in their calamities." Psa. cxli. 5.

He visited all parts of his land, promoting true godliness ; appointing judges in all the principal cities, with a supreme court at Jerusalem, admonishing them to act " in the fear of the Lord, faithfully, and with a perfect heart." " Take heed what ye do :" was his counsel, " for ye judge not for man, but for the Lord, who is with you in the judgment. Wherefore now let the fear of the Lord be upon you ; take heed and do it : for there is no iniquity with the Lord our God, nor respect of persons, nor taking of gifts," 2 Chron. xix. 6, 7. This advice should ever be borne in mind by the christian. His Master approves not of slothful or timid servants ; and those are in woful error who refrain from acting with decision, thinking that they may thereby win golden opinions from men, and be estimated as oracles of wisdom, when in fact all their aim, however they disguise it, is their own ease, and a good word from their fellow-mortals. Let us avoid precipitate and injudicious conduct, but never let us think to please God by avoiding the active duties of the station where we are placed. The 82nd Psalm contains advice similar to that of Jehoshaphat, and has been attributed to this period.

Ahaziah, the successor of Ahab, reigned only two years over Israel. Jehoshaphat was induced to join him in a commercial expedition to Ophir, reviving the trade so advantageous to Solomon, but which apparently had been discontinued by his successor. At that time Edom was under the control of Judah, though a separate government. The ships had scarcely left their port on the Red Sea, when they were wrecked. A prophet reproved Jehoshaphat for thus joining Ahaziah. The king of Judah listened to the warning, and refused to allow the king of Israel to join in another voyage with a similar design.

The reign of Ahaziah in Israel was shortened by an untimely end. A railing, or lattice work, gave way, and he fell from a gallery, or from the flat roof of his palace. Finding the effects of the injury he had received increase, he sent messengers to inquire of Baalzebub, the god of Ekron, whether he should recover. This wretched deity retained his honours even to the days of our Lord, and the malevolent Jews attributed the miracles of the Saviour to this satanic influence. Elijah confronted the messengers with a warning of the certain death of the idolatrous monarch. Two bands of soldiers were sent, one after the other, to seize the prophet, but, at his call, fire from heaven consumed the wicked scoffing instruments of an ungodly king. A third leader humbly addressed the prophet in the language of supplication. He prevailed, and Elijah stood before the king, and warned him of his approaching end, stating that he should not come down from the raised part of the room where he was laid ; this place now is called the divan, and is represented in drawings of eastern manners. The prophet showed that he was not concerned for himself, but for the honour of Jehovah.

Ahaziah was succeeded by his brother Jehoram, who removed a part of the worst idolatries of his father ; and Jehoshaphat was again persuaded to unite his forces to those of Israel, and that for an object in which the interests of the latter were concerned more than his own. It is sad to see so good a man repeatedly forming unhallowed alliances, after repeated reproofs

and warnings. The expedition was to reduce the king
of Moab, who was tributary to Ahab, but on the death
of that monarch he threw off the yoke of Israel. The
king of Edom joined them, and the confederate forces
took the direction of the wilderness of Edom, to attack
the southern border of Moab. After seven days'
march in this wilderness, they were in great distress
for want of water. The idolatrous king of Israel was
in despair, but Jehoshaphat sought for a prophet who
could inquire of the Lord for them. Elisha was at
hand, and the kings went to him. This prophet, who
had accompanied the army unnoticed by the leaders,
told Jehoram to have recourse to the prophets of his
father and mother, but declared his willingness to attend to Jehoshaphat as a servant of Jehovah. Through
his intercession, a miraculous supply of water was procured. The Moabites were deceived by the appearance of water where none had previously existed, and
the shining of the sun giving it a red appearance, they
thought it was blood, and that the kings had smitten
each other, and they rushed forward to the spoil. The
Moabites were defeated, and fled; and their country
was devastated. Their king sacrificed his own son as
an offering to the devil-gods whom he served, thus
showing his desperation and deadly resolution against
the invaders. The Israelites retired homeward.

The last event recorded of the reign of Jehoshaphat
is the deliverance from an invasion of the Moabites,
who were assisted by the Ammonites and other confe-
derated tribes from the wilderness. The invasion was
very formidable, and a public fast was proclaimed, Jehoshaphat pleading for the nation in an earnest prayer,
recorded in 2 Chron. xx. 6—12. An answer of encouragement was given by a prophetic impulse upon Ja-
haziel, a Levite; and Jehoshaphat led forth his army
towards the wilderness of Tekoa, with this short but
comprehensive address, " Believe in the Lord your
God, so shall ye be established ; believe his prophets,
so shall ye prosper ;" and they marched forward sing-

ing praises to the Lord. An answer was speedily sent.
Discord arose among their enemies ; the children of
Lot destroyed the children of Esau, and then attacked
each other, so that when the army of Judah gained the
heights which commanded a view of the position of the
invading forces, they beheld a widely-spread mass of
slaughter, and had only to descend to the spoil, which
employed them three days to gather. They afterwards
assembled and offered thanksgivings to the Lord, and
returned to Jerusalem with solemn rejoicings.   The
115th and 46th Psalms are ascribed to this event.
The result of the invasion is stated ; it was not a common occurrence : the fear of God was on all the neighbouring nations, when they heard how Jehovah fought
against the enemies of his people.   This is the last
event recorded respecting Jehoshaphat.   He slept with
his fathers, after a prosperous reign of twenty-five
years, and was buried in the royal sepulchres.

About two years before the death of Jehoshaphat,
Elijah was summoned from this world, and his departure was attended with circumstances unknown before
or since.   Enoch, indeed, like Elijah, was translated,
and saw not death, and was not found, because God
had translated him ; but the particulars attending
Enoch's removal from this world are not related.

Elijah was at Gilgal, when he learned that the hour
of his departure was at hand. He desired to bid farewell to the disciples at Bethel, and then to be alone.
But Elisha determined on no account to leave his beloved master.   There was earnest desire for solitude
on the one part, and the firm resolve, on the other, not
to lose sight of his spiritual father while in this world.
God saw fit that there should be human witnesses of
the glorious translation of Elijah, both near and at a
distance.   This brings to our notice the schools of the
prophets at Bethel and Jericho. It appears, that from
the time of the decline of the priesthood in Israel, a
succession of prophets was raised up, a body of men not
selected from any peculiar rank or particular tribe, nor

set apart by any especial rites, but men who devoted
themselves to religious exercises under some leading
pious character; and who lived in a community, labour-
ing for their maintenance in the honourable occupation of tillers of the soil; going forth when opportunity offered, as preachers of righteousness, and at
times charged by the Holy Spirit with some prophetic
intimation or prescient warning. This was the active
ministry of Israel and Judah in the time of the kingdoms, and doubtless was made useful to the awaken-
ing of many careless souls, while it left others without
excuse. The first notice of such institutions occurs in
1 Sam x. but they are frequently mentioned in the
later historical books, and in the prophetic writings.
The disciples at Bethel and Jericho were aware of
the approaching removal of Elijah, and this made
Elisha more strongly resolved not to leave his master,
while a number of the sons of the prophets followed
at a distance, to see what would come to pass.

The river Jordan owned the Divine control, and its

waters separated to allow the prophets to pass on dry

ground. The mantle of Elijah had no innate virtue
or miraculous power, but, like the rod of Moses, it
was a symbol of the authority committed to the prophet. Elijah told Elisha to make his last request, and
he asked for a double portion of his master's spirit ;
for, being called to fill his place, he knew the need of
a like spirit. While conversing together, and their
communing could not have been of ordinary matters,
there appeared some wondrous form, described as " a
chariot of fire, and horses of fire ; it parted them asunder ; and Elijah went up by a whirlwind into heaven."
Such is the Scripture narrative, and it is best given in
the very words of the Bible. We need not inquire
into particulars which are not revealed, and which
human reason cannot explain. It is sufficient for us
to be assured as to Elijah, that his mortality was
swallowed up of life, and that his corruptible nature
put on incorruption.

Elisha caught the mantle of the ascending prophet,
as it fell towards the ground. It was a token that the
spirit and power of Elijah rested on Elisha. The sons
of the prophets admitted this, when they saw the
stream of Jordan again parted before him. Still they
could not be fully satisfied that Elijah had ascended
to a heavenly mansion ; during three days they
searched the country around, but they sought for him
in vain. Elisha was called upon to work another
miracle. He healed the waters of Jericho. Water is
a common mercy ; the enjoyment of it is too little
prized : but if withheld, or if it is unwholesome, then we
feel our necessity, and learn to prize the blessing
hitherto neglected or despised. And is it not so with
the waters of life ? When placed in a neighbourhood
where the ministrations of the word abound, few
rightly estimate them ; but in a barren and thirsty
land, the soul has longing desires to commune with its
God as in the days that are past.

Elisha proceeded to Bethel. Youths and young men
came forth and mocked the prophet ; they alluded

with ribald tongues to the ascension of Elijah, and
applied to his successor the epithet of "bald head,"
then, as now, one of the most opprobrious terms used
in the east, and as such now often applied to the mis-
sionary, though his head may be covered with hair.
This was an insult to the God of Elijah and Elisha : the
prophet turned and denounced the Divine judgment
these children were bringing upon themselves.   Two
bears rushed from the wood, and the mocking crowd
hastened to escape ; but the beasts, with fury beyond
their usual nature, tore forty-two of these wicked
children.

JEHORAM, or JORAM.

REIGNED EIGHT YEARS.

[B. C. 904—896.]

THE son of Jehoshaphat succeeded to the throne of
Judah ; but he widely differed from his father.   His
character and conduct resembled that of his relative
by marriage, of the same name, who reigned in Israel
at the same time.   Jehoram of Judah married Athaliah, the daughter of Ahab.   This union led him to do
evil in the eyes of the Lord.   The first act of his
reign showed that he was a thoroughly wicked character ; he caused his six brothers to be murdered,
though they were provided for by their father, and do
not appear to have done any thing to excite his jealous fears.   Idolatry and licentiousness were next
introduced, and the kingdom was soon weakened and
disordered.   The wickedness of rulers, generally, is
punished without long delay.   The Edomites revolted
from the dominion of Judah, and thus a stop was put
to the traffic of the east ; and Libnah also threw off
the yoke.   The Philistines, and the southern Arabs,

ravaged the land, and even plundered Jerusalem, carrying some of the royal family into captivity. The king himself was smitten with a painful internal disease, and died after two years of suffering, thus ending a wicked and inglorious reign of eight years. The people made no demonstrations of respect for his memory ; " he departed without being desired." No one valued Jehoram while he lived, no one lamented him when dead. Early in his reign Jehoram had been warned of the Divine judgments, by a writing which came to him from the prophet Elijah, probably written by that prophet not long before his death, and which appears to have been the first instance of a written prophecy like those which form so considerable a part of the sacred books.

AHAZIAH, or JEHOAHAZ.

REIGNED ONE YEAR.

[B. C. 896.]

AHAZIAH, the youngest son of Jehoram, succeeded his father as king of Judah, his elder brethren having been slain by the invaders. He also followed the evil courses of the house of Ahab, which soon ended in his destruction. He came to the throne at the age of twenty-two, and joining with his brother-in-law Joram, of Israel, was slain with him at Samaria. Here we must notice the events in Israel during the reign of Joram, or Jehoram, who succeeded to that throne a few years before the death of Jehoshaphat, and was contemporary with Jehoram and Ahaziah, of Judah. They are recorded with minuteness, and contain much that is interesting to believers of all ranks and stations in life.

Joram, or Jehoram, of Israel, the son of Ahab, wrought evil in the sight of the Lord, but not like his

L

father and his mother, for he put away the image of
Baal, yet he cleaved to the sins of Jeroboam. The
Moabites rebelled against him, and he subdued them
by the aid of Jehoshaphat, as already related, but was
afterwards involved in war with the Syrians. The
translation of Elijah to heaven also has been noticed ;
we have now briefly to refer to Elisha, the successor
of that powerful prophet. He prayed that a double
portion of Elijah's spirit might rest upon himself ; this
was manifested by the remarkable miracles he was enabled to perform, and by his decided testimonies against
wicked rulers, although he was not called to act precisely in the same course. The course of Elijah may
be compared to the mighty tempest which rives the
sturdy oaks, and hurls the craggy rocks from the
mountain top ; that of Elisha to the steady, yet forcible gale, which dissipates noxious vapours on the land,
and enables the mariner rapidly to plough the surface
of the deep.

The miracles of Elisha are recorded in the early
chapters of the Second Book of Kings. The particulars bring before the reader many interesting circumstances connected with the private life of that period ;
but especially they show the repeated warnings which
were sent to rebellious Israel. They were acts of
merciful charity, while they showed the Almighty
power of that God whom the nation had forsaken and
defied. We can only briefly enumerate them here.
Elisha healed the waters at Jericho ; he multiplied
the widow's oil ; restored to life the son of the Shunammite ; healed the poisonous food which was set before the sons of the prophets ; multiplied a small present of first fruits, so as to suffice a hundred men ;
healed the leprosy of Naaman, the Syrian general ;
and showed the direct interference of Providence in
the daily concerns of life, by causing the iron axe-
head to swim. The list may be concluded with a
statement from the Jewish book of Ecclesiasticus,
" The spirit of Elijah rested upon Elisha ; while he

lived he was not moved with the presence of any
prince, neither could any bring him into subjection :
nothing could overcome him, and after his death his
body prophesied. He did wonders in his life, and at
his death his works were marvellous." Or rather the

Elisha multiplying the widow's oil. See page 110.

work of God was marvellous, for it was the Divine
power alone that conveyed life into a dead body,
which touched the prophet's bones. The wonders
wrought by the prophet Elisha were seals to the mis-
sion of Elijah, and kept in remembrance the true faith
and worship of God in an idolatrous generation. The
words of the men of Shunem, 2 Kings iv. 23, show
that public worship of prayer and praise was held on
the new moons and sabbaths, by the prophet. The
notices respecting the sons of the prophets exhibit a
pleasing picture of communities dedicated to the service of God, but not living in monkish seclusion, or
indolence. The verses of *Newton* bring the scene
before our view, and convey useful instruction by way
of improvement on the history :—

The prophets' sons in times of old,
Though to appearance poor,
Were rich without possessing gold,
And honoured though obscure.

The reader can peruse the remainder of these lines.

The healing of Naaman caused heathens to acknowledge that there was no God in all the earth but
Jehovah, while the miraculous punishment of Gehazi
showed that the Lord was "a jealous God," almighty,
and determined to vindicate the Divine honour, and
to manifest that his mercy is without price.

In the restoring to life the son of the Shunammite,
we recognize the power of Him who triumphed over
death, and who could not be held captive by the grave.

We must pass on to instances which show how the
Spirit of the Lord wrought with Elisha in matters of a
public nature. The deliverance of the kings in their
expedition against Moab has been noticed; other instances refer to the contests between Israel and Syria:
for Joram was continually involved in hostilities with
that neighbouring power. The Syrian plans of warfare
were frequently disclosed by the prophetic knowledge
imparted to Elisha; this being known to the enemy,
troops were sent to Dothan to seize the prophet, and
at dawn the city was surrounded by horsemen and chariots of war. The attendant of Elisha hastened to his
master with the intelligence, and was permitted to see
the efficacy of the prophet's weapon—prayer! He had
a glimpse afforded him of "a greater army from the
skies," the ministering spirits that wait on the heirs of
salvation, then commissioned to protect the successor
of Elijah. But this was not all; some miraculous effect
upon the eyesight of the Syrians placed them at the
disposal of the prophet, and when their perfect vision
was restored, they found themselves in the midst of
Samaria. At the request of the prophet, they were
permitted to depart, and the account they gave satisfied
their king that it was of no avail to make any attempt
against the person of Elisha.

Benhadad besieged Samaria not long afterwards.

In those days the methods of attack on fortified places were very imperfect; the siege was protracted, and the city was reduced to such extremity by famine, that two women agreed to kill and eat their own children. One fulfilled the compact; but when the other was called upon to furnish her supply for the like horrible repast, nature's better feelings prevailed—she hid her child, and the other monster hesitated not to complain to the king of this breach of their agreement! Such sufferings had been foretold, Lev. xxvi. 29, by Moses, among the judgments to be expected for national crimes. The king of Israel, like many, who are convinced of sin yet are angry against others rather than themselves, threatened the life of Elisha. A messenger, or executioner, was sent to put the prophet to death, but he was stayed at the door, by Elisha's desire, to wait the coming of his master, who was following him. Joram came, and manifested his convictions; he exhibited a mind apparently struggling with an imbittered spirit, till he was ready to give himself up to despair. But the prophet, when the king entered, declared that there should be the greatest plenty in the city on the following day, personally warning a courtier who derided the prediction, that he should see the plentiful supply, but should not partake thereof.

That night the Syrian army was panic-stricken by a noise like that of the approach of a mighty host—by the effect of a Divine terror upon their minds. They left their camp standing, and fled away in haste; the intelligence was brought to the city by some lepers who had been shut out beyond the walls, agreeably to the Divine command to Moses; and the Israelites hastened to the pursuit, but with a degree of caution which shows that in ancient as in later days, it was not unusual to tempt an enemy by a feigned retreat and abandonment of the cantonments of an invading army. The plunder of the camp was brought to the gates, and stores of wheat and barley were sold for trifling sums. The lord whom the prophet had warned, being appointed to keep order at the gate, saw this, but he was trodden to death by the famished crowd, who eagerly thronged forth to obtain food. How uncertain are life and its enjoyments! how certain are the Divine threatenings!

About the twelfth year of Joram, Elisha went to Damascus. Benhadad was sick, but he ordered the prophet to be received by his principal officer with honour, and inquiry to be made of him as to the result of his disease. A long procession, with presents, met the prophet; he returned an ambiguous answer, but expressly spoke of Hazael as the successor to the throne, and as likely to act with savage fury towards the Israelites. Hazael received this declaration with surprise, and expressed a sense of his own insignificance. On the morrow Benhadad died; it is not clearly stated, whether by the murderous hand of Hazael, or by the inadvertence of that officer, or by his own undesigned act, in drawing over his face a thick cloth saturated with water, used in the east to produce coolness and keep away the insects. The result, however, was in conformity to the word of Elisha. The minister was raised to the throne.

Shortly afterwards, Hazael invaded Israel, and Joram was wounded in battle, and returned to Jezreel to be healed; here he was joined by Ahaziah, king of Judah. At this time Elisha sent one of the sons of the prophets to Ramoth-gilead, near which place the army of Israel was then encamped, with directions to anoint one of the captains, named Jehu, and to deliver a message, commissioning him to execute the Divine judgments against Ahab's family. The young man performed his office, and hastened away. The peculiar appearance of the young prophet excited the inquiry of the other captains. On learning what had passed, they placed Jehu on the top of the outer stairs which led to the entrance of the tower, and proclaimed him king.

Jehu then hastened to Jezreel. The kings heard of the suspicious manner of his approach, and went forth

2

to meet him ; they met at the portion of Naboth, when
Joram, ascertaining the hostile intentions of his captain, turned to flee, but was pierced by Jehu with an
arrow, and his dead body was thrown into the plot of
ground that had belonged to the murdered Israelite,
agreeably to the denunciation which Jehu recollected
having heard Elijah utter in that very place.   Ahaziah
fled, and escaped to Samaria, but Jehu arriving there
shortly after, caused search to be made for the king
of Judah : he again escaped, but was seen by Jehu,
who directed him to be pursued ; after he had received
a mortal wound, his charioteer still pursued his course,
and reached Megiddo, where Ahaziah died.

On Jehu's arrival at Jezreel, Jezebel adorned herself, coloured her cheeks, or tinged her eyelids, according to the practice of the east.   These artificial colour-
ings always have been practised by abandoned characters.   She went to the window fronting the street, from
whence she reproached Jehu, who, calling to know
whether any of the attendants took his part, directed

her to be thrown down, and caused his horses to tram-
ple her under foot.   Having gone into the palace, and

taken refreshment, he directed that the remains of Jezebel should be interred ; but the word of the Lord had
literally been fulfilled—she had been eaten of dogs, only
a few bones remaining. Her carcass had been de-
voured by these hungry animals; they roam about
eastern cities in large numbers, owning no master, but
devouring the offal and carrion, which otherwise would
be left to encumber the streets and highways.

Jehu pursued his course, as an executioner of the
Divine judgments. The descendants and kinsmen of
Ahab and Ahaziah were put to death. Jehu then,
having collected together the worshippers of Baal,
caused them to be put to death, and destroyed the idol
temple. So far Jehu showed himself jealous for the
honour of Jehovah, but he did not give up the false
worship of Jeroboam. The death of Ahaziah recalls
our attention to the affairs of Judah. Both kingdoms
had lost their rulers, and this is a period by which the
chronology of each can be examined and ascertained.

JOASH.

REIGNED FORTY YEARS.

[B. C. 889–849.]

A SCENE of blood was exhibited at Jerusalem as well
as at Samaria, but of ambition, not of judgment. Athaliah, the daughter of Jezebel, hearing of the death of
Ahaziah, put her grandchildren to death, and seized
the throne of Judah. One infant was saved by his aunt,
the wife of the high priest, who concealed him six years
in the private chambers of the temple. The usurping
queen reigned for that period, during which she and her
adherents plundered and injured the temple, and built a
house for Baal, and established idolatrous worship. In
the seventh year, Jehoiada, the high priest, concerted
a plan for the restoration of the lawful king ; and on

the sabbath, when a double number of Levites and
priests were in attendance, he armed them from the
weapons placed in the temple by David, and bringing
out the infant monarch, placed the crown upon his
youthful brow, and the book of the Divine law in his
hand.   He then anointed Joash, and all the people
shouted, " God save the king !"   Athaliah heard the
joyful outcries, and hastening into the temple, saw the
cause.   Her exclamations of " treason" were silenced
by the command of Jehoiada, who directed that she
should be taken out of the temple courts and put to
death, as she deserved.

Jehoiada made a covenant, whereby himself as the
high priest, the young king, and the people, were engaged to serve the Lord.   The continuance of idolatry
rendered necessary this ·renewal of the covenant between the king and the people, to rule and to be ruled
in the fear of the Lord.   *Josephus* notices the obliga-
tions between the kings of the Jews and the people.
A mutual engagement in the Divine fear, is the best
assurance for the faithful discharge of our duty, and
this solemn covenant was followed by the destruction
of idolatry, and the re-establishment of the worship of
Jehovah, according to the law of Moses ; then all the
people of the land rejoiced, and the city was quiet:
" when the righteous bear rule, the city rejoiceth."

Jehoiada was an upright and pious character, and
trained the young king in the ways of piety, which he
manifested at an early age.   The temple had been
erected 350 years, and had suffered not only by the
lapse of time, but by the destructive proceedings of
Athaliah and her adherents.   The building was dear
to Joash from early recollections ; it was the place
where he had been sheltered from death, and had
passed his first years.   But the instructions of Jehoiada
doubtless gave the temple stronger claims to his regard,
and he then could use the language of the psalmist,
" How amiable are thy tabernacles, O Lord of hosts :

a day in thy courts is better than a thousand." He
urged the priests to collect money throughout the land
to repair the house of the Lord ; the sums directed to
be paid, Exod. xxx. 13, and Lev. xxvii. 3 ; and also
free contributions ; but the priests and Levites hastened not the work, and in his twenty-third year Joash
called them before him, and after reproaching their neg-
ligence, made another arrangement, whereby other
methods should be employed, more diligence used in
gathering the money, and also more system observed
in expending it.   Even Jehoiada appears to have been
remiss in this work : it is an evil sign when the priests
of the Lord are reluctant to repair the breaches which
time and ill-designing men have made in the goodly
fabric, the outward church of Christ ; but it is still
worse when they " daub it with untempered mortar,"
are satisfied with presenting a glossed and merely
smoothed surface to the world, being contented that
matters go on in quietness, though the structure is
hastening to decay.   The work proceeded ; Jehoiada
and the king's officers acted in harmony, and " the
workmen dealt faithfully ; " materials were purchased,
and the repairs and needful works completed.

This favourable state of affairs did not continue very
long.   Jehoiada died at the great age of 130 years ;
after his death the king allowed the princes of Judah
to lead him into idolatry.   Being warned by Zechariah, the son of Jehoiada, of the consequence of forsak-
ing the Lord, the people conspired against the faithful
witness, and at the king's instigation, or with his con-
nivance, the prophet was stoned in the court of the
temple !   This atrocious act was followed by speedy
punishment.   Hazael invaded Judah ; and the Syrian
army, though comparatively few in number, defeated a
large force of the Jews, plundered the temple, committed great havoc, and slew the wicked princes.
Disease came upon the king, and while in this state he
was slain by a conspiracy of his servants, whose names

are recorded as the sons of idolatresses ; a proof that men do not secure even worldly friendship by patronizing the votaries of error.

About the time that Joash began his earnest efforts for the repair of the temple in Judah, Jehu, king of Israel, died. Though especially selected to execute the commands of Jehovah, he did not turn from the evil ways of Jeroboam, and the Lord began to cut Israel short. Hazael was permitted to be successful in his warfare around Israel. He attacked the Philistines and the kingdom of Judah ; the tribes on the east of Jordan also suffered much. Jehu died, after reigning twenty-eight years, and was succeeded by his son Jehoahaz, who followed the evil courses of his father, though he did not wholly deny the authority of Jehovah. The Lord therefore permitted the Syrians to prevail against Israel during the whole of this reign, so that Jehoahaz was brought very low ; yet some degree of deliverance appears to have been afforded to his people after a time. This king died a short time before Joash of Judah, and was succeeded by his son Jehoash.

AMAZIAH.

REIGNED TWENTY-NINE YEARS.

[B.C. 849—820.]

THE first act of Amaziah, the son of Joash, when he succeeded to the throne of Judah, was to put to death his father's murderers ; but it is noticed that he attended to the Divine injunction, Deut. xxiv. 16, and did not put the children to death with their parents, which was, and still is, the general practice among eastern nations in the case of great offenders. His conduct appears in the main to have been influenced by the fear of God ; but, it is said, " not with a perfect heart." Where religion is merely countenanced, and not made the ruling principle, there will be little satisfaction, either to the individual or to those connected with him. The kingdom of Judah evidently began to decline after the murder of the son of Jehoiada. To this height of wickedness, when the blood of the priest was mingled with the blood of the sacrifices, Hosea is considered by some to allude, iv. 2 ; when speaking of the sins of the land, as causing the Lord to have a controversy with the inhabitants, he says, " And blood toucheth blood." From this period, the declension of the kingdom of Judah may be dated, though for a time it was spared, and many invitations to repentance sent by prophets.

About the twelfth year of his reign, Amaziah invaded Edom. His preparations for this expedition were on a large scale, and he hired a considerable number of the subjects of Israel to assist. A prophet warned him not to trust in this aid, for the Lord was not with Israel ; but if he confided in the Divine power, God would give him the victory. Amaziah at first hesitated, considering that the money he had engaged to pay for the aid of these forces would be lost ; but the prophet reminded him, " The Lord is able to give thee much more than this." Let not the important truth be forgotten. Every one is, sooner or later, called on to make sacrifices for the Lord's sake ; and he can give more in return, and will do so if it is for the good of those who make the sacrifice ; nothing is ever lost by giving up sunday trading, or any species of unhallowed gain. We may also remark, that Amaziah does not appear to have hesitated to fulfil his bargain with the Israelites, though so disadvantageous to himself. Amaziah went forth with his own people, and was victorious, but his success led him astray ; he cruelly drove his Edomite prisoners over the precipices, which are numerous in their land. He yielded to sin and folly, by bringing home the idols of the conquered people, and setting them up to be his gods. When warned by a prophet against the absurdity of adopting the gods which, as he had himself seen, were utterly worthless as protectors, he silenced the faithful minister, and threatened him.　Sad is the condition of those who thus turn away from attending to the messengers of the Lord.

Impiety leads to presumption ; the disappointed and dismissed forces of Israel committed some ravages on their return homewards, and Amaziah sent a boasting message to Jehoash, king of Israel, challenging him to battle.　The king of Israel sent a reply couched in a parable, but conveying a cutting though polished sarcasm on the presumption of Amaziah.　But the latter would not hear; it was of God, that he might suffer for his idolatry and pride, and he was defeated and taken prisoner.　The conqueror broke down a part of the wall of Jerusalem, and pillaged the temple and the palace.　Amaziah reigned several years afterwards, when a conspiracy being made against him, he fled to Lachish, and was there slain.

The victory of Jehoash over Amaziah, shows that the state of the kingdom of Israel was much improved. The cause of this is stated in 2 Kings xiii.　We there read of the last sickness and death of Elisha, and that while the prophet was on his death-bed, Jehoash, the king of Israel, came and lamented over him as "the chariot of Israel, and the horsemen thereof."　Cavalry and armed chariots, in that day, were the most powerful forces brought into the field ; of these the Jewish nation were destitute ; but the prayers of their prophets and holy men supplied more efficient aid for the battle.　By Elisha's direction, the king prepared his bow, and the aged prophet was raised in his bed, to lay his hands on the king's hands.　The window was opened, and the arrow winged its flight eastward.　The king was commanded to smite the ground with the remaining arrows.　He did not enter into the meaning of the sign with that earnestness which might have been expected: he smote the ground thrice, and then stayed. The prophet reproved this want of zeal, but promised

M

him three victories, which were gained over the forces of the son of Hazael. This lowering the power of Syria, enabled Jehoash to pursue his contest with Judah.

Soon after the defeat of Amaziah, Jeroboam, the second of that name, succeeded to the throne of Israel. There was some outward improvement, and the Lord was pleased to grant farther deliverance to Israel by him, and an interval for repentance was given to the nation. The reign of Jeroboam II. lasted forty-one years. At this time Jonah was called forth as a prophet. He spoke of the deliverances to be afforded to Israel; but all that we have of the personal history of this prophet is preserved in the book of Jonah, which teaches how wrong and dangerous it is to shrink from any work which God calls us to perform. We also see the Lord's mercy, in sparing the king and people of Nineveh upon their repentance; and a notable miracle, in the preparing of the fish to swallow the disobedient prophet, and his preservation within that fish, which shows that the laws of nature are subject to the Divine will. This also furnished a remarkable type of the short abode of Christ in the grave, Matt. xii. 39, 40.

UZZIAH.

REIGNED FIFTY-TWO YEARS.

[B. C. 809—757.]

UZZIAH, or Azariah, was only five years old when his father, Amaziah, was slain ; he did not begin to reign till sixteen years of age, when the people made him king. Of the state of Judah during this interregnum of eleven years we have no account ; but that such an interval of regency, or unsettled government, did occur, *Usher* and *Hales* have shown from Scripture statements.

Jeroboam II. king of Israel, died B.C. 793. He recovered the district east of Jordan, and enlarged his dominions to the north, by conquests from the Syrians, extending even to Damascus. During his reign lived the earliest of the prophets, whose writings have come down to us. Hosea foretold the judgments soon to come upon Israel, describing their idolatries in strong figurative language ; but, like all the prophets, his views were carried forward, not only to the coming of the Saviour in the flesh, but even to later days. Amos also spoke of the judgments to come upon the house of Jeroboam, and it is expressly stated, that he prophesied two years before the great earthquake. Amos, viii. 8, 9, seems to declare that this earthquake should be accompanied by an eclipse of the sun. *Usher* shows, that an eclipse, nearly total in Judea, took place two years after the death of Jeroboam, so that Amos prophesied in the last year of that king. He was a simple herdsman, a gatherer of sycamore fruit, or wild figs, but was directed by the Lord to leave his flock, and to give prophetic warnings of approaching judgments. Three plagues of a fearful kind were denounced as about to be inflicted without delay : one, the earthquake already noticed. Another, the swarms of lo-

custs and other insects, which were to be such as had
never before been seen; this dreadful destruction,
causing the harvest to perish and the trees to wither,
also is described in very forcible language by Joel.
The third plague was a drought, accompanied by fire
from heaven, which burned up the pastures and foliage. Amos denounced woe to those who were at
ease in Zion, and trusted in the mountain of Samaii ',
Amos vi. 1. He gave warning of approaching invasions
and captivities, as well as of the judgments upon the
fruits of the earth. He spoke of the lamentations as
being general through the land, and in particular that
" in all vineyards shall be wailings," a forcible expression, which cannot be fully entered into, except by those
who have witnessed the universal joy which prevails
during the season of vintage. These denunciations
were not pleasing to the ears of the courtly idolatrous
divine, the priest of Bethel. He warned Amos not to
prophesy there any more, for it was the king's chapel
and the king's court; but to flee away to Judah, and
eat bread there. From which we may suppose, that
while the rough manners and faithful addresses of the
prophets rendered them unacceptable to worldlings,
like the king of Israel and his court, they were better
treated in Judah, where the king sought the Lord.
Amos saw in vision the destruction of the idolatrous
temple of Samaria. See Amos iii. 14, to ix. 5.

The reign of Uzziah was long and prosperous. In
the early and middle part especially, he was attentive
to the Divine will, wherein he had been instructed by
a prophet named Zechariah. He prevailed against
the Philistines, the Arabians, the Ammonites, and the
Edomites; he obtained access to the Red Sea, and
built Elath, rendering it again a suitable station for trade
with the east. He was attentive to the security of his
dominions, and fortified Jerusalem. His character exhibited traits not often united— he was skilled in the art
of warfare, yet he "loved" the peaceful occupations
of husbandry; this expression plainly intimates that

agriculture had his preference, and was encouraged by him. The murderous scenes of warfare cannot be pleasant to any one who seeks God aright.

It is distinctly stated, that the Divine help made Uzziah thus strong; yet he was lifted up, and pride must have a fall. Though he made himself strong and formidable to the surrounding nations, the prophets warned him of the approaching overthrow of the kingdom by foreign powers. Uzziah also sinned grievously by a direct violation of the Divine institutions. He was not satisfied with the kingly power, nor with the liberty every one possesses to worship the Lord in spiritual acts of prayer and praise. He desired to perform some of those ceremonial rites, which by the law were confined to the descendants of Aaron, and to assume the high priest's office, of burning the incense on the golden altar. The priests boldly withstood the king, and while he persisted in the act, and was wroth with them, he was struck with leprosy, and they thrust him out of the temple; nay, self-convicted, and impressed by this miraculous infliction, he hastened forth, and from that day to the time of his death he dwelt in a separate house, as the law concerning lepers, Lev. xiii. 46, directed. During the latter part of his reign, Jotham, his son, governed as regent, and the land enjoyed peace and rest. It may be remarked here, that the regular computation of the Olympiads, which were periods marked by the regular recurrence of public games, celebrated every fourth year at Olympia, in Greece, began to be used during the reign of Uzziah, as an era for chronology; they commence B. c. 776, from that period the history of other nations may with greater certainty be connected with that of Israel.

We must again return to Israel. After the death of Jeroboam ii., a long interregnum of twenty-two years followed, of which there is no account, unless Hosea is to be considered as delineating the state of Israel during this interval. Dark indeed is the picture, and it was applicable to both the kingdoms—" There is no

M 2

truth, nor mercy, nor knowledge of God in the land.
By swearing, and lying, and killing, and stealing, and
committing adultery, they break out, and blood toucheth
blood." "The revolters are profound to make slaughter,
though I have been a rebuker of them all." "As for
Samaria, her king is cut off as foam upon the water."
The cause is assigned—"My people are destroyed for
lack of knowledge; because thou hast rejected knowledge, I will also reject thee." Even the priests are described as murdering in the way by consent. The fatal
sentence is passed: "Ephraim is joined to idols; LET
HIM ALONE," Hosea iv. 17. Awful is the state of those
who are, like Israel, left to themselves!

Zachariah, the son of Jeroboam, at length was raised
to the throne of Israel, but his reign was short and
evil. After six months, he was murdered by Shallum,
who usurped the throne, and in a month he was, in his
turn, slain by Menahem, who reigned ten years, and
treated with brutal cruelty those who refused to acknowledge his authority. This unsettled state of affairs encouraged an invasion from the mighty power of Assyria,
and Put, the monarch of Nineveh, was induced, by a
sum of money, to confirm Menahem in the kingdom of
Israel. His son, Pekahiah, reigned only two years,
when he was murdered by Pekah, the son of Remaliah,
who reigned in his stead. The government of Israel
was now evidently become wholly military; gained by
violence, and maintained by force.

This brings us to the last year of Uzziah in the kingdom of Judah, and that year is rendered remarkable
by the designation of Isaiah to the prophetic office.
His vision, and the glorious appearance of Deity,
which he was permitted to behold, are recorded, Isa. vi.
He gave warning of approaching judgments, yet closed
with assurances of mercy.

Of the period just noticed, it should be said, that Judah and Israel had been permitted to enjoy an interval of comparative rest and repose for nearly half a
century; but storms rapidly approached, and warnings

of direful events were sounded in the ears of kings and
people. Internal troubles began to rise ; and " coming
events cast their shadows before." Joel's prophecies at
this time have been already mentioned ; he warned
of approaching desolations by famine and the sword, and
called for fasting and supplication, that the Lord
might spare his people, and not give his heritage to reproach, that the heathen should rule over them ; wherefore should they say among the people, " Where is
their God ?" The exact fulfilment of the denunciations
of this prophet, which related to the judgments accomplished at that period, would call the attention of his
hearers forcibly to the latter part of his prophecy,
which evidently referred to the times of the Messiah,
and extends even to a period not yet arrived. How
awful the scenes depicted by Joel, iii. 9—21, to which
it is generally believed we have yet to look forward !

> Ye angels thrust the sickle in,
> The world is now matured in sin,
>   The press is full, the fats o'erflow ;
> The Lord's decisive day is near,
> And countless multitudes appear
>   Before his judgment-seat below.
>
> The sun shall set in endless night,
> The moon and stars withdraw their light,
>   The shatter'd earth's foundation groan,
> The ruin'd heavens his wrath shall feel,
> And nature's last convulsions tell,
>   That Israel's Strength remains alone,

The earliest portion of the prophecies of Isaiah, iii.
2—5, are deeply interesting. He begins by declaring
that, " the day of the Lord of hosts shall be upon
every one that is proud and lofty, and upon every one
that is lifted up ; and he shall be brought low." The
prophet goes on to speak of the judgments then immediately at hand. A painful delineation of the confusion which comes by sin is given ; the oppression of
the rulers, and the vanity and pride of the Jewish fe-
males are graphically described. *Boothroyd* renders
the latter part, with the additional knowledge now possessed, as to eastern customs, as follows :—

" In that day will the Lord take from them
The ornaments of the feet-rings,
And the net works, and the crescents,
The pendants, and the bracelets, and the thin veils;
The tires, and the fetters, and the zones,
And the perfume boxes, and the amulets;
The rings and the jewels of the nostril;
The embroidered robes and the tunics,
And the cloaks, and the little purses;
The transparent garments and fine linen vests,
And the turbans and the mantles." Isa. iii. 18—23.

The circumstantials of the description may differ, but the proud daughter of ancient Zion and the modern belle of Europe, are equally distant from the adorning with modest apparel, with shamefacedness and sobriety, taught by Scripture.

The state of Judah is represented under the parable of a vineyard, Isa. v., an illustration very striking, as constantly present unto the minds of a people, whose vineyards clothed the fruitful hills in every direction. That period was one of outward prosperity in many respects ; buildings arose on every side, and feasting was the business of the day, while they regarded not the work of the Lord, neither considered the operation of his hands ; but they were warned, that he would call the nations from afar, to devastate the land, and darkness and sorrow should cover it. We find that the strongest denunciations of Divine judgments often were made when all appeared at rest, and no immediate danger threatened. And thus Israel speaks in warning to other nations. Let us not dwell on the luxuries and arts, and improvements of our day, but inquire whether the accelerated pace at which some circumstances of outward prosperity move on, should not cause us deeply to consider the case of Israel, and to receive admonitions from her example and her fate.

O Israel, of all nations most undone!
Thy diadem displac'd, thy sceptre gone—
Cry aloud, thou that sittest in the dust,
Cry to the proud, the cruel, and unjust;
Knock at the gates of nations, rouse their fears,
Say, Wrath is coming, and the storm appears.

JOTHAM.

REIGNED SIXTEEN YEARS.

[B. C. 757—741.]

JOTHAM succeeded his father as king of Judah, when twenty-five years old. He had governed the land for some years as regent, in consequence of the leprosy of Uzziah, and was among the good monarchs of Judah. His reign was prosperous. Jotham became mighty, because he established his ways before the Lord his God. He built a new gate to the temple, and improved the adjacent part of Jerusalem. He also built in other parts of the land, and prevailed against the Ammonites, who paid him a considerable tribute, both in money and in corn. But the warnings of the prophets were still sounded in the ears of the people, and the voice of Micah was heard, " Arise ye, and depart ; for this is not your rest : because it is polluted, it shall destroy you, even with a sore destruction." And, in a series of denunciations against many cities and places in the land, whose names were expressive of the troubles about to come, the prophet gave warning of approaching captivity. Especially, it was declared that Samaria should be as a heap of the field, for her wound was incurable. See Micah i. ii.

During the reign of Jotham, B. C. 753, Rome was founded ; that city by whose power Jerusalem ultimately was destroyed. This is clearly ascertained, both by history and astronomy ; an eclipse of the sun occurring on the day of the foundation of that city, and one was visible at Rome, July 5, in that year. In the latter part of this reign hostilities again began between Israel and Judah. It is remarkable how few particulars are given of some of the longer reigns, while, as in the histories of Elijah and Elisha, the inspired historian seems to have been directed to dwell minutely on the events of shorter periods, and those of a description which the world would rather have

passed by.   In the modern histories of England, how
many pages are unprofitably occupied with the details of campaigns by land, and combats by sea, while
the more glorious triumphs of the ministers of Christ,
who, during the same period, have prominently stood
forward in their Divine Master's cause, who have
boldly attacked the strong-holds of Satan, and carried
the spiritual warfare into the heart of his kingdom, are
passed by, or noticed in contemptuous phrases.   But
the Lord seeth not as man seeth.   The Elijahs and
Elishas of our times will be remembered, when generals, admirals, and ministers of state are forgotten ; to
the former only can it be said with truth,

> Servant of God ! well done ;
> Rest from thy lov'd employ,
> The battle fought, the victory won,
> Enter thy Master's joy.
>
> Soldier of Christ, well done ;
> Praise be thy new employ ;
> And, while eternal ages run,
> Rest in thy Saviour's joy.

AHAZ.

REIGNED SIXTEEN YEARS.

[B. C. 741—725.]

A DARKER cloud now came over Judah as well as Israel. Ahaz was an idolater, worse than any preceding
king of Judah. He offered sacrifices to idols, and
even sacrificed his infant children.   In the early part
of his reign, Pekah king of Israel, and Rezin king of
Syria, proceeded to invade Judah, intending to place the
son of Tabeal on the throne of David ; who he was is
not stated in Scripture, but he seems to have been
some factious Jew. The confederate kings prevailed
at first ; each defeated the army of Judah, and Pekah
carried away captive a vast number of men, women,
and children. But when the captives were brought to

Samaria, the prophet Oded went forth, and reproved
the leaders of Israel for their design to make slaves of
their brethren.   His words prevailed, the captives
were clothed and refreshed, and sent back to their
own land.   The confederates again advanced, and
even besieged Jerusalem.

Isaiah was then directed to take his infant son, whose
name was significant—Shear-jashub, meaning " a remnant shall return," and to go to meet Ahaz, while engaged in preparing for the defence of the city.   He
declared the will of the Lord, that Rezin and Pekah
should not succeed in their design, comparing them to
two firebrands nearly burned out, and exhibiting
smoke rather than flame, Isa. vii. He encouraged the
idolatrous king and his people, when their hearts were
moved with fear, " as the trees of the wood are moved
with the wind," to turn to Jehovah, and trust in his
promises.   But Ahaz refused to ask a sign as the prophet counselled, excusing himself that he would not
tempt the Lord.   It is easy for those who are resolved
not to *trust* God, to offer as an excuse that they will not
tempt him !   Yet the prophet gave a sign, which was
to confirm the hearts of those who feared the extinction
of the royal line of David, by declaring that the Messiah should be from the family of Ahaz, and which also
would confirm the faith of future ages, by its expressly
predicting the miraculous birth of Christ.   He further
declared, that both Israel and Syria should be deprived of the kings who now caused such apprehension
to Ahaz, before the infant child, then with the prophet,
knew how to distinguish good from evil—by the time
he was three or four years old.   The prophet was then
led to predict the desolate condition to which the land
should be reduced, even to be covered with briers and
thorns, through that very power of Assyria, to which
Ahaz had sent for aid in the present extremity.   At
the close of Isa. vii. the desolation to which Judah
would be reduced is shown, by the description of a
country deprived of its inhabitants, and left to become

wild. The cultivated land overrun with briers and
thorns, the pastures so abundant from the want of cattle to feed therein, that a cow and two sheep would
supply a family with milk, and the few inhabitants supported by that pastoral diet and the wild honey, instead
of attempting to cultivate land ; the face of the country
so overrun with wild animals, that the people would go
armed for their defence, and obtain food by the chase.

But the dimness and the darkness, it is stated, should
disappear before the day-spring from on high.   The
words, Isa. ix. 1, 2, are expressly applied to the preaching of Christ in the region of Galilee.   "That it might
be fulfilled which was spoken by Esaias the prophet,
saying, The land of Zabulon, and the land of Nephtha-
lim, by the way of the sea, beyond Jordan, Galilee of
the Gentiles ; the people which sat in darkness saw great
light ; and to them which sat in the region and shadow
of death light is sprung up," Matt. iv. 14—16. The destruction about to come upon Israel is described
by imagery familiar to that agricultural land ; the cutting down of the people should be like the reaping of
corn in the fertile valley of Rephaim, and the few that
should remain are compared to the gleaning grapes,
which are left after the main crop has been plucked ;
and to the few olive berries on the uppermost boughs,
beyond the reach of those who gather the fruit.

In his extremity, Ahaz had recourse to the king of
Assyria, and in order to procure the assistance of that
monarch, he sent him all the gold and silver which he
could collect from his treasury and from the temple.
Tiglath-pileser, king of Assyria, received the treasure
sent by the king of Judah, and marched against Syria ;
thus causing a diversion in favour of Ahaz. He took
Damascus and slew Rezin, but his aid was not effectual ; he did not assist against the Edomites and the
Philistines, who took advantage of the distressed state
of Judah, and occupied the south and east of the land.

The first chapter of the prophecies by Isaiah gives
a painful but forcible delineation of the state of Judah,

at that time, just after it had been traversed by the invading armies. " Your country is desolate, your cities are burned with fire ; your land, strangers devour it in your presence, and it is desolate, as overthrown by strangers." Then noticing the weakened state of the glorious city of Jerusalem, he proceeds, " And the daughter of Zion is left as a cottage in a vineyard, as a lodge, (or shed,) in a garden of cucumbers, as a besieged city." The Edomites in particular appear to have been ready, as in former times, and at a later period, to take advantage of the distressed state to which Judah was reduced.

The temporary relief afforded by the Assyrians tended to continue the distress of the land, by the contributions and presents necessary to satisfy this new friend, while two lasting mischiefs resulted from the new state of things. Instead of two princes of comparatively small power, with whom Judah was able to cope, the kingdom had one mighty prince for its immediate neighbour, against whom no effectual resistance could be made. The conquest of Damascus also placed Elath, the eastern port of the Red Sea, in the power of Assyria, as a part of the kingdom of Syria, Rezin having taken it from Judah not long before. This finally excluded the Jews from the profitable commerce they had carried on with the countries bordering on the Indian ocean, and caused the inland traffic, or transmission of these commodities towards the west, to be carried in a different direction. The loss of an advantageous trade tended to weaken the kingdom of Judah. The intercourse with the Assyrian monarch led Ahaz farther in evil courses. He went to Damascus to meet Tiglath-pileser, who had taken that city and carried away the inhabitants as captives, and while there his attention was attracted by the altar of an idol, and he had a pattern of it sent to his priest at Jerusalem, to have one made like it. On this, after his return, he offered his sacrifices, causing the original brazen altar of the temple to be thrown aside, as an

N

object of no value, or merely to be kept for use on occasions of particular emergency. The folly of idolatry
is too glaring to need much remark; the kings and
princes of Israel and Judah, in those times, appear to
have changed their objects of worship, and attendant
ceremonies, with the same levity and fickleness that influence alterations as to the fashions of dress and furniture in our days. Such is the practice of many heathen nations even now; and the choice and rejection
of the local and tutelary saints of popery is very similar: a new picture, or image, of the virgin Mary at-
tracts votaries to one place, while an old one is disre-
garded in another. Ahaz also made other alterations
in the ornaments and utensils of the temple, and removed the "covert for the sabbath," a place to shelter the people while engaged in the spiritual worship
of prayer and praise, or when listening to the discourses
of the prophets on the sabbath and solemn days.
Idolatry of every kind desecrates the sabbath.

The triumph of Israel over Judah was short. The
king of Assyria carried away captive the tribes beyond
Jordan, and some of the inhabitants north of Israel.
This was the first captivity. Pekah himself fell by a
conspiracy instigated by Hoshea, in the fourth year of
Ahaz; a second interregnum, or state of confusion, ensued, which lasted ten years, and was then ended by
the throne being occupied by Hoshea, three years before the death of Ahaz, of whose inglorious reign no
farther particulars are given; but it is recorded that
they brought him not into the sepulchres of the kings.
It would appear from this, and other passages, that
there was some system of examining the actions of
their kings—honouring or disgracing their memories
according to their deserts. This was customary in
Egypt, and a similar plan evidently was practised in
Judea, at least in some instances.

Warnings were again given by the prophets Hosea
and Isaiah; the latter seems expressly to testify against
the false security of the rulers of Judah at that time.

" Wherefore hear the word of the Lord, ye scornful men,
That rule this people which is in Jerusalem.
Because ye have said,
We have made a covenant with death,
And with hell are we at agreement ;
When the overflowing scourge shall pass through, it shall not
    come unto us :
For we have made lies our refuge,
And under falsehood have we hid ourselves ;
Therefore thus saith the Lord God,
Behold, I lay in Zion for a foundation a stone,
A tried stone, a precious corner stone, a sure foundation :
He that believeth shall not make haste.
Judgment also will I lay to the line,
And righteousness to the plummet :
And the hail shall sweep away the refuge of lies,
And the waters shall overflow the hiding place.
And your covenant with death shall be disannulled,
And your agreement with hell shall not stand ;
When the overflowing scourge shall pass through,
Then ye shall be trodden down by it."   Isa. xxviii. 14—18.

In the end it will be found that all events have been
wisely directed by Him who " is wonderful in counsel,
and excellent in working." In the verses which follow,
the diversified ways in which the Lord is pleased to
deal forth his judgments are stated, and illustrated by
agricultural processes.

" For his God doth instruct him to discretion,
And doth teach him.
For the fitches are not threshed with a threshing instrument,
Neither is a cart wheel turned about upon the cummin ;
But the fitches are beaten out with a staff,
And the cummin with a rod.
Bread corn is bruised ;
Because he will not ever be threshing it,
Nor break it with the wheel of his cart,
Nor bruise it with his horsemen."   Isa. xxvi. 26—28.

The last days of the kingdom of Israel were now
close at hand, and it is affecting to trace the manner in
which the unwillingness of the Lord to give up his people is described in many passages, but in none more
than in Hosea xi. The concluding verse notices the
light which yet shone upon Judah :—

" Ephraim compasseth me about with lies,
And the house of Israel with deceit :
But Judah yet ruleth with God,
And is faithful with the saints."   Hosea xi. 12.

See page 144.

HEZEKIAH.

REIGNED TWENTY-NINE YEARS.

[B. C. 725—696.]

WE now come to the most important reign among the
successors of Solomon, that of Hezekiah. "Like
unto him was there no king before him, that turned to
the Lord with all his heart, and with all his soul, and
with all his might, according to all the law of Moses;
neither after him arose there any like him." His confidence was placed wholly and fully in the Lord his
God. He clave to the Lord, and departed not from
following him.

In the first days of his reign he opened the temple,
and, assembling the priests and Levites, charged them
to cleanse and set in order the house of God without
delay. Immediately after this was done, the king sacrificed sin-offerings and burnt-offerings, and also presented
services of prayer and praise. "The thing was done
suddenly," but "God had prepared the people," so

that they brought more sacrifices than the priests were able to offer. Hezekiah then summoned the people to Jerusalem to keep the passover, and sent messengers through Israel as well as Judah, to make known his intention of solemnizing this festival. Many derided the invitation, but others were wiser, and a very great congregation assembled at Jerusalem. The people removed the altars and idols, and were even more ready than the priests and Levites. Every particular enjoined by the law could not be observed, but Hezekiah prayed, "The good Lord pardon every one that prepareth his heart to seek God, the Lord God of his fathers, though he be not cleansed according to the purification of the sanctuary." The prayer was accepted, as the prayer of the humbled and returning sinner ever will be. A large number of sacrifices were offered, and the Divine blessing sought and granted.

The people showed their faith by its fruits. They destroyed the images, and high places, and groves, throughout the land. Among the objects of worship then destroyed, was the brazen serpent which Moses had set up in the wilderness, which had been preserved as a memorial of mercy, but it had become a symbol of the serpent-worship, or devil-worship of the heathen ; and Hezekiah caused it to be broken to pieces, calling it Nehushtan, "a piece of brass ;" thus reminding the people that they were not to rest upon any outward symbols. Yet, strange to tell, notwithstanding this indisputable account of the destruction of the brazen serpent, the romanists even lately pretended to exhibit it in the church of St. Ambrose, at Milan, among other superstitious relics ! What a proof of the extent to which that church has carried the exclusion of the Bible from the people at large. Another church in the same city, not to be inferior in point of ancient judaical relics, exhibited what was said to be a part of the rod of Aaron ; while a whole rod, also claiming to have belonged to the first high-priest, was exhibited at Rome !

Hezekiah provided for the due celebration of spiritual

worship, and for the general instruction of the people, circulating among them the proverbs of Solomon, and other sacred records. In 2 Chron. xxxi., we have an account of the willingness with which the people contributed to this good work, the support of the reformed and renewed temple services. This willingness came from the Lord, who alone can induce the heart of man to contribute to his service. If at any time a general unwillingness to assist what appears to be a good work is found to prevail, it is well for the conductors to examine whether they are not pursuing a wrong course, for the Lord will not forsake his own works.

Hezekiah, having removed all that was opposed to Divine worship in Judah, went forward with courage; he prevailed against the Philistines, and refused to be subject to the king of Assyria. He restored the regular worship of the sanctuary, and the people were forward in making free-will offerings for its due support, to a very considerable extent; so that, during four successive months, they were adding to the heaps of the first-fruits of the produce of the soil. The great work of reformation seems to have been promoted by the discourses and prophecies of Micah, who bears testimony against the apostacy and cruelty of the princes, and the falsehood of the priests and prophets, who "teach for hire, and divine for money," yet inducing the people to rest in false confidence. For their sakes, especially, should Zion be plowed as a field, and Jerusalem become heaps, and the mountain of the house (the temple and its courts) be as the high places of the forest, barren and desolate. But the people were encouraged by assurances of the restoration and future glory of their nation, and especially by the concluding words of the prophet, which called to personal as well as national repentance.

" Who is a God like unto thee,
That pardoneth iniquity,
And passeth by the transgression of the remnant of his heritage ?
He retaineth not his anger for ever, because he delighteth in mercy.
He will turn again, he will have compassion upon us ;

He will subdue our iniquities;
And thou wilt cast all their sins into the depths of the sea.
Thou wilt perform the truth to Jacob,
And the mercy to Abraham,
Which thou hast sworn unto our fathers from the days of old."
Micah vii. 18—20.

An important period of history now comes under notice. The first universal monarchy, that of Assyria, was at its height, and was involved in warfare with Egypt, still a mighty power. In these contests other neighbouring nations engaged ; and Canaan, from its central situation between the contending powers, was often the immediate occasion, and sometimes the 'seat of war. The prophecies of Isaiah and of Micah, delivered at this time, show the general agitation which then prevailed among the different powers, and the destruction about to fall successively upon them, while the clearest prophecies of the Messiah were set forth by Micah, in which the despised village of Bethlehem was expressly pointed out as the birth-place of Him that should be Ruler in Israel; and the Tower of Edar, the Shepherd's tower, was noticed as the place for the announcement of these glad tidings.

Hoshea, king of Israel, imprudently formed an alliance with Egypt, and refused to continue tributary to Assyria. But the Egyptians did nothing to assist Israel ; they acted to that kingdom, and afterwards to Judah, according to the words spoken by Isaiah ; they gave no assistance ; but were as a broken reed. In the fourth year of Hezekiah, Shalmaneser, the king of Assyria, besieged Samaria and took it, after a tedious siege of three years. Then was " Woe to the crown of pride, to the drunkards of Ephraim." Samaria, beautiful in its situation and rich in its fertility, was utterly cast down. The Assyrian, unconscious that he was only "the rod of Jehovah's wrath," and that the instrument of correction would be broken and cast aside, when the child had been sufficiently corrected, and its services were no longer required, devised a course to break the power of Israel. He caused the survivors of the seven tribes, settled between Jordan and the sea, to be carried away

to a remote part of his dominions, far to the east, where
it is considered that many of their descendants still
continue. This had been expressly foretold by the
prophet Amos.

The causes for this captivity of Israel are stated at
length, 2 Kings xvii. 7—23, where the justice of the
Divine judgments is fully vindicated, while the sins of
Israel and the extent to which they carried their idolatry, are strikingly delineated.

" For so it was, that the children of Israel had sinned against the
Lord their God, which had brought them up out of the land of Egypt,
from under the hand of Pharaoh king of Egypt, and had feared other gods,
and walked in the statutes of the heathen, whom the Lord cast out
from before the children of Israel, and of the kings of Israel, which they
had made. And the children of Israel did secretly those things that
were not right against the Lord their God, and they built them high
places in all their cities, from the tower of the watchmen to the fenced city.
And they set them up images and groves in every high hill, and under
every green tree: and there they burnt incense in all the high places, as
did the heathen whom the Lord carried away before them ; and wrought
wicked things to provoke the Lord to anger: for they served idols,
whereof the Lord had said unto them, Ye shall not do this thing. Yet
the Lord testified against Israel, and against Judah, by all the prophets,
and by all the seers, saying, Turn ye from your evil ways, and keep my
commandments and my statutes, according to all the law which I
commanded your fathers, and which I sent to you by my servants the
prophets. Notwithstanding they would not hear, but hardened their
necks, like to the neck of their fathers, that did not believe in the Lord
their God. And they rejected his statutes, and his covenant that he
made with their fathers, and his testimonies which he testified against
them ; and they followed vanity, and became vain, and went after the
heathen that were round about them, concerning whom the Lord had
charged them, that they should not do like them. And they left all the
commandments of the Lord their God, and made them molten images,
even two calves, and made a grove, and worshipped all the host of
heaven, and served Baal. And they caused their sons and their daughters to pass through the fire, and used divination and enchantments,
and sold themselves to do evil in the sight of the Lord, to provoke him
to anger. Therefore the Lord was very angry with Israel, and removed
them out of his sight: there was none left but the tribe of Judah only.
Also Judah kept not the commandments of the Lord their God, but
walked in the statutes of Israel which they made. And the Lord rejected all the seed of Israel, and afflicted them, and delivered them into
the hand of spoilers, until he had cast them out of his sight. For he
rent Israel from the house of David; and they made Jeroboam the son
of Nebat king: and Jeroboam drave Israel from following the Lord,
and made them sin a great sin. For the children of Israel walked in
all the sins of Jeroboam which he did; they departed not from them ;
until the Lord removed Israel out of his sight, as he had said by all his
servants the prophets. So was Israel carried away out of their own
land to Assyria unto this day." 2 Kings xvii. 7—23.

Even now, in India and other heathen lands, the emblem of some idol may be seen "in every high hill, and under every green tree" that is remarkable for size and beauty.

In the latter part of the same chapter there is an account of the colonies of the heathens who were settled by Shalmaneser in the promised land, and their suffering from the wild beasts of the field, which the Lord caused to multiply in the depopulated territory. This led to a partial adoption of that mutilated worship of Jehovah practised by the followers of Jeroboam, still further debased by the worship of idols; "they feared the Lord, and served their own gods." How true a description of many a nominal christian at the present day! he has an undefined, uncertain fear of the Lord, which brings torment, and not solace; he seeks for comfort in the things of the present world, but seeks in vain.

At this time Nahum appears to have delivered his prophecy. He belonged to one of the ten tribes, and probably found a refuge in Judah, where he was inspired to declare "the burden of Nineveh," and minutely to describe the way in which that proud city, the capital of Assyria, should fall. It was then a metropolis at the height of commercial prosperity and military renown, whose merchants were multiplied above the stars of heaven, and whose captains were as the grasshoppers, both numerous and destructive; but all should flee away, and their place not be known. The very site of Nineveh was unknown for ages, and even now it is pointed out by *Rich* and others, as only distinguished by a few grassy mounds, but with much uncertainty. Not one monument of royalty, or token of splendour, remains; the very ruins have perished! With what energy the prophet predicts the utter desolation to come upon the destroyers of his country!

After the conquest of Israel, Shalmaneser directed his victorious course to the northward, and spent five years in warring against Syria, and in a long and un-

successful siege of Tyre, which he undertook at the
instance of the Philistines. His failure rendered the
Tyrians for a time secure and insolent; but Isaiah,
chap. xxiii., warned them of the destruction which
should come upon their state; then, carried forward
by the prospects into futurity which were opened to his
view, he also foretold its restoration, and even that
holiness to the Lord, which was realized when, in the
early part of the christian era, the followers of Christ
were numerous within the walls of Tyre.

In the fourteenth year of Hezekiah, Sennacherib,
the son and successor of Shalmaneser, invaded Judah,
when Hezekiah submitted to him, and purchased peace
by the payment of a considerable sum, to raise which
he was obliged to strip off much of the gold plating
which adorned the temple. The proud Assyrian received the money, but stayed not his course. He proceeded to attack the southern fortified cities of Judah
to open his way to Egypt. Still Hezekiah and his
people were not left destitute of support. The ultimate destruction of the proud victorious Assyrian was
plainly foretold, Isa. x., and when these enemies had
been compared to the lofty cedars of Lebanon, and it
had been declared that the thickets of the forest should
be cut down with iron, and the high ones of stature be
hewn down, even the house of Judah for a time be laid
prostrate, yet while the oaks and cedars were torn up by
the root, never again to grow—the promised Deliverer
should be seen as a rod or slender twig, springing out
from the stem or stump of Jesse, and as a branch growing out of his roots. And the prophetic eye beheld
that happy day when none shall hurt or destroy in
all the holy mountain, for the earth shall be full of the
knowledge of the Lord as the waters cover the sea.
The beautiful hymn of praise, Isa. xii., would be particularly delightful at this time to those who looked
forward with faith in the Divine promises.

At this juncture Hezekiah fell sick, but was mira-
culously restored, after he had been warned to prepare

for death.   He earnestly prayed that his life might be
spared under the critical circumstances in which his
country was then placed.   His removal also would have
affected the direct lineal succession to the throne of
David, for Hezekiah was childless at that time.   Of
his recovery a miraculous sign was given, the shadow
of the sun being caused to return on the large dial
which marked the passing hours in the palace.

Sennacherib sent three generals to form the siege of
Jerusalem, threatening destruction, and offering removal to Assyria as the only alternative to the inhabitants.   Hezekiah had strengthened Jerusalem, which
was almost impregnable from its situation.   He secured
the water-courses, raised the wall, and threw up outer
embankments, repaired the citadel of Millo, in the strong-
holds of Zion, and provided weapons in abundance.

> " Thou didst look in that day to the armour of the house of the forest.
> Ye have seen also the breaches of the city of David, that they are
> many :
> And ye gath red together the waters of the lower pool.
> And ye have numbered the houses of Jerusalem,
> And the houses have ye broken down to fortify the wall.
> Ye made also a ditch between the two walls for the water of the old
> pool :
> But ye have not looked unto the maker thereof,
> Neither had respect unto him that fashioned it long ago."
> Isa. xxii. 8—11.

But Hezekiah trusted not in his own might, nor did
he rely, like Israel, upon the aid of Egypt.   He listened
to the warning of the prophet,

> " Woe to the rebellious children, saith the Lord,
> That take counsel, but not of me ;
> And that cover with a covering, but not of my Spirit,
> That they may add sin to sin :
> Therefore shall the strength of Pharaoh be your shame,
> And the trust in the shadow of Egypt your confusion." Isa. xxx. 1, 3.

Thus if Isaiah referred to this invasion, and not to the
latter siege by Nebuchadnezzar, his words are to be applied to the people and the princes, not to the king.

Hezekiah interceded for the people, and an answer
of encouragement was given, with an assurance of the

disappointment of the invader. Sennacherib was un-
successful in his invasion of Egypt, and, hearing that
the king of southern Arabia was advancing to intercept
his return, he marched towards Jerusalem, and sent a
boasting letter to Hezekiah. This the pious monarch
carried to the temple, and spread before the Lord with
solemn prayer; a message of triumphant encouragement was sent in return. The moment was critical,
the approach of Sennacherib is described by Isaiah :

> " He is come to Aiath, he is passed to Migron ;
> At Michmash he hath laid up his carriages:
> They are gone over the passage :
> They have taken up their lodging at Geba ;
> Ramah is afraid ;
> Gibeah of Saul is fled.
> Lift up thy voice, O daughter of Gallim :
> Cause it to be heard unto Laish,
> O poor Anathoth.
> Madmenah is removed ;
> The inhabitants of Gebim gather themselves to flee.
> As yet shall he remain at Nob that day :
> He shall shake his hand against the mount of the daughter of Zion,
> The hill of Jerusalem." Isa. x. 28—32.

The consternation of Jerusalem is graphically described,
Isa. xxii. 1. But though permitted to approach close
to Jerusalem, Sennacherib shot not an arrow against
the holy city. A miraculous blast was sent upon him ;
in one night 185,000 of his army were struck with
death, "the branch of the terrible ones was brought
low." " The Assyrian fell with the sword, but not of
a mighty man ; and the sword, not of a mean man, de-
voured him." Thus weakened, Sennacherib returned
to his own land, and there was murdered by his own
sons, while at worship in an idol temple.

> The Assyrian came down like the wolf on the fold,
> And his cohorts were gleaming in purple and gold ;
> And the sheen of their spears was like stars on the sea,
> When the blue wave rolls nightly on deep Galilee.
>
> Like the leaves of the forest when summer is green,
> That host with their banners at sunset were seen ;
> Like the leaves of the forest when autumn hath blown,
> That host on the morrow lay wither'd and strown.

During this interval of apprehension, and while the
invader appeared ready, as it were, to swallow up the
small remnant of the Jewish nation, the prophet Isaiah
was inspired to deliver some of the most powerful and
energetic of his prophecies : chapters xiii., xiv., xxiv.,
to xxvii., are assigned to this period. The three latter
chapters appear to us particularly sublime, when taken
in connexion with these times of trial. The inspiring
nature of these communications must especially be
borne in mind, carrying the hearer and the reader on
to a time of trial, far more severe than that which
accompanied the Assyrian invasions. In what strong
language this is described! " The earth shall reel to
and fro like a drunkard, and shall be removed like a
cottage ; and the transgression thereof shall be heavy
upon it ; and it shall fall, and shall not rise again."
Here is reference also to that day when death will be
swallowed up in victory, and the Lord God will wipe
away tears from off all faces. How consoling, under
these circumstances, the gracious invitation,

> " Come, my people, enter thou into thy chambers,
> And shut thy doors about thee :
> Hide thyself as it were for a little moment,
> Until the indignation be overpast.
> For, behold, the Lord cometh out of his place
> To punish the inhabitants of the earth for their iniquity :
> The earth also shall disclose her blood,
> And shall no more cover her slain." Isa. xxvi. 20, 21.

Also chapters xxix., xxx., xxxi., are applicable to the
same events ; there it was shown that " as birds flying,
so will the Lord of hosts defend Jerusalem ; defending
also he will deliver it ; and passing over he will preserve it." Nor are these, and the many similar gracious
assurances in other passages, confined to that period.
Let those who, through Divine grace, are members
of the spiritual Jerusalem, rejoice in that name, and say,

> Glorious things of thee are spoken,
> Zion, city of our God !
> He, whose word can not be broken,
> Form'd thee for his own abode :

o

On the Rock of ages founded,
What can shake thy sure repose;
With salvation's walls surrounded,
Thou may'st smile at all thy foes.

Saviour, if of Zion's city
I through grace a member am;
Let the world deride or pity,
I will glory in thy name:
Fading is the worldling's pleasure,
All his boasted pomp and show;
Solid joys and lasting treasure,
None but Zion's children know.

The Babylonians, and other vassals of Assyria, took
advantage of the weakened state of their oppressors,
and revolted. The king of Babylon, impressed by the
miraculous recovery of Hezekiah, and the deliverance
of the Jews, sent ambassadors to congratulate the Jewish monarch. Hezekiah, elated by success, showed the
ambassadors his treasury, not emptied by the forced
contributions to the Assyrians, but filled by his recovered wealth, and by the spoil of the destroyed army.
We read that at this moment God left Hezekiah to try
him, and to show to him, and to all who read the sacred
history, the evil which is in the heart of man. The king
and his people do not appear to have been duly sensible
of the necessity of ascribing simply to God all the
mercies and deliverances they had received, and this
brought just displeasure upon them; it added to the
evils by which the measure of their iniquity was
nearly filled. The prophet Isaiah was sent to declare
that the wealth and spoil the ambassadors had seen,
should very soon become the prey of their king, and
be carried to Babylon. Hezekiah was sensible of his
sin, and humbled himself before the Lord, with thankfulness for the sparing mercy promised to be vouchsafed during his own times.

Other nations brought presents to Hezekiah, and the
kingdom prospered all his latter days. He executed
several works for the benefit of his people; among
them was one of considerable magnitude for supplying
Jerusalem with water. But among the chief ornaments

and blessings of the reign of Hezekiah were the discourses, sermons, and prophecies of the evangelical prophet Isaiah. Many of these refer to the approaching events relative to Babylon, Egypt, and other powers. The chapters xxxii. and xxxiii. are thought to allude to the recovery of Hezekiah ; but if so, the prophet, as elsewhere, is soon carried on to contemplate Him, who alone can be " a covert from the tempest ; as rivers of water in a dry place, as the shadow of a great rock in a weary land." Connected with this are the remarkable prophecies, chap. xxxiv., xxxv., addressed to all nations, which contain denunciations of Divine vengeance against the enemies of the people of God, and predict the flourishing state of his church after these judgments shall be executed, when "the ransomed of the Lord shall return, and come to Zion with songs and everlasting joy upon their heads : they shall obtain joy and gladness, and sorrow and sighing shall flee away."

Repeated and clear declarations concerning the Messiah are given, and also full statements of the blessings and privileges of the gospel. The powerful language of the inspired prophet strikes the reader forcibly even now, under all the disadvantages of a translation, and with much difference as to times and manners ; how great must have been the effect upon the people, when delivered with all the power of gifted speech, and enforced by attendant circumstances. Let us, for instance, imagine the costly aqueduct completed, and all Jerusalem crowding to see the wished-for supply, rejoicing in the free gift of this needful blessing. The prophet is there, Divine inspiration comes over his soul, he calls aloud,

" Ho, every one that thirsteth,
Come ye to the waters ;
And he that hath no money—come ye, buy, and eat ;
Yea, come, buy wine and milk
Without money and without price.
Wherefore do ye spend money for that which is not bread ?
And your labour for that which satisfieth not ?
Hearken diligently unto me, and eat ye that which is good,
And let your soul delight itself in fatness.

Incline your ear, and come unto me :
Hear, and your soul shall live ;
And I will make an everlasting covenant with you,
Even the sure mercies of David." Isa. lv. 1—3.

This subject would lead us far beyond the limits of
the present work, but we must not proceed without
noticing the historical accuracy, and the minuteness of
the prophecies, those of Isaiah especially. The precise
and literal fulfilment of the predictions he was inspired
to utter, respecting the neighbouring nations, is visible at
the present day.   Babylon, Tyre, Egypt, Idumea, and
other countries, are precisely in the state in which the
book, written 2500 years ago, describes they should be
brought into ; while many circumstances are preserved
by the prophets, which throw such light upon obscure
portions of history, that an accurate account of the
events connected with the downfal of the various
nations, might be drawn from the predictions delivered
when many of them were in their high and palmy
state ; indeed many, even of the more minute circumstances, are only preserved in the prophetic writings.
If the reader is not already acquainted with the work
of Keith on the fulfilment of prophecy, he is earnestly
recommended to peruse that valuable book, in which
all the needful information on the subject is brought
into a small compass with surprising minuteness of
detail, and the whole is applied to the great end for
which the predictions of the seers were preserved, to
show to succeeding generations, that the testifying of
Jesus is the spirit or drift of prophecy.   How clear the
prediction of his sufferings, chap. liii., how glorious the
description of his final triumph, chap. lxiii.   And how
beautiful the delineation of the blessings of gospel
times in other passages, especially where the Saviour's
healing maladies of the soul is expressed by language
descriptive of his miracles in curing bodily ailments.
    The beautiful lines of Pope will be remembered,

The Saviour comes! by ancient bards foretold ;
Hear him, ye deaf; and all ye blind behold !
He from thick films shall purge the visual ray,
And on the sightless eye-ball pour the day ;

'Tis he the' obstructed paths of sound shall clear,
And bid new music charm the' unfolding ear:
The dumb shall sing, the lame his crutch forego,
And leap exulting like the bounding roe,
No sigh, no murmur, the wide world shall hear,
From every face he wipes off every tear.
In adamantine chains shall death be bound,
And hell's grim tyrant feel the' eternal wound.

The most remarkable portion of the prophecies of Isaiah are from chap. xl. to lxvi. Many parts may be applied to the captivity at Babylon, and the joyful return from thence; but these are lost in the great events to which they were preliminary or typical. Various divisions of these discourses have been suggested, which assist in rendering them more clearly; but none perhaps is more worthy of notice than that of *Fraser*, who considers that these chapters give several parallel views of the period from the first promulgation of the gospel, unto that establishment of the kingdom of the Messiah in the world, to which the believer still looks forward with joyful anticipation. These parallels he arranges as follows :—1. Chap. xl. and xli. 2. Chap. xlii. to xlviii. 3. Chap. xlviii. to lii. ver. 12. 4. Chap. lii. ver. 13, to lx. 5. Chap. lx. to lxiv. 6. Chap. lxv. 7. Chap. lxvi.

Certainly there is nothing similar in existence to these twenty-seven chapters. Through the whole the Lord, as the Creator, the Messiah, and the Redeemer, speaks as directly from himself, and addresses his people in every succeeding generation.

Psalm xliv. is assigned to this period, and considered as referring to the blasphemy of Rabshakeh while Psalms lxxiii., lxxv., lxxvi., are thought to describe the destruction of the army of Sennacherib.

Judah rapidly recovered from the depressed state to which it was brought by the ravages of the Assyrians. In 1 Chron. iv. we find that the Simeonites so much increased, both in their own numbers and that of their cattle, that they took possession of a part of Arabia adjoining Palestine. In 2 Chron. xxxii., the prosperity of the latter part of Hezekiah's reign is described: not only was he wealthy in gold, silver, and jewels, but als oin agricultural produce, flocks, and herds. " God had given him substance very much," " he prospered in all his works," and we know that " the blessing of the Lord maketh rich, and he addeth no sorrow with it." But a darker day for Judah was at hand.

Hezekiah's life was prolonged fifteen years, agreeably to the Divine word sent to him by the prophet during his dangerous illness. He then departed in peace, and was buried in the " chiefest" of the sepulchres of the sons of David. He received an honourableb urial, suited to the glories of his reign. The sepulchres here mentioned, it is supposed are an elaborate work which still exists to the north of Jerusalem, and which was cut in the solid rock at a vast expense both of time and labour, and which is the only actual remains of ancient Jerusalem that can now be traced satisfactorily. A passage leads to an open court, excavated in the rock, about forty yards square, on one side of which is a porch, once beautifully ornamented, but now much defaced. From thence are entrances which lead into several smaller rooms cut in the rock, with recesses for bodies, and places for sarcophagi, fragments of which, richly carved, still remain. These rooms were closed with stone doors, carved in pannels, one of which *Maundrell* found still upon its hinge, or rather turning upon a tenon which rested in a socket in the floor. Annexed is a representation of this last vestige of the kings of Judah in its present state. This, then, is the place of which Hezekiah said, " I shall go to the gates of the grave :" of this he said, " the grave cannot praise thee." Here he was laid, after he had been permitted for fifteen years to " go up to the house of the Lord," and whatever may have become of his dust, he has experienced the truth of the words of that gifted seer, who prophesied in his courts, and declared that there is One who has ransomed his people from the power of the grave.

See page 154.

MANASSEH.

REIGNED FIFTY-FIVE YEARS.

[B. C 696—641.]

The longest and most wretched reign in the kingdom
of Judah followed the bright days of Hezekiah. There
had, it is true, been an outward reformation, and doubtless many turned to the Lord, worshipping him in
spirit and in truth ; but the depravity of the rulers of
Judah was not removed. Manasseh succeeded to the
throne of his father at the early age of twelve years.
Surrounded by evil counsellors, he turned to do evil in
the sight of the Lord, reviving the abominable rites
which Hezekiah had caused to cease. Altars for
Baal, and groves for Ashtaroth, again abounded in the
land, and the worship of the host of heaven was carried
on even within the courts of the temple. The royal
children were sacrificed or dedicated to Moloch, the
serpent worship and divination were restored, a graven

image was placed in the house of the Lord ; these abominable rites led to acts of the deepest depravity, and even to persecution and murder.

Under these proceedings it is generally supposed that Isaiah was martyred. The Shebna, mentioned Isa. xxii. 15, it is thought, was the same Shebna the scribe, who filled the office of secretary in the days of Hezekiah, but who, on the adoption of idolatry by Manasseh, obtained the office of treasurer, displacing Eliakim. The passage in Isaiah, just mentioned, seems to exhibit Shebna, full of pride and luxury, anxious to prepare a conspicuous sepulchre, a mark of high rank in the east, by which persons thought to procure fame for themselves while alive, and more than common remembrance after death. While superintending this work, the prophet apparently drew near, and addressed the proud apostate in the words recorded, declaring the disgrace and destruction which awaited the unhappy Shebna, and the restoration of Eliakim. This it is thought was the last prophecy of Isaiah. Jewish traditions relate that he was seized, and sawn asunder with a wooden saw, a lingering and painful death.

The atrocities of Manasseh speedily brought that destruction upon Jerusalem, which was described as evil that would cause the ears of the hearer to tingle. The like fate with that of Samaria and the house of Ahab was threatened, and the awful result was thus emphatically declared, " I will wipe Jerusalem as a man wipeth a dish, wiping it, and turning it upside down." An expressive delineation of Jerusalem, as it was literally emptied of its inhabitants by the final captivity of the land. Many years afterwards, the crimes of Manasseh, " that which he did in Jerusalem," are mentioned as a primary cause of the Jews being removed into all the kingdoms of the earth, Jer. xv. 4.

The following are the closing particulars of Manasseh's history. In the twenty-second year of his reign, the Assyrians invaded Judah, and were successful, for the glory and the defence of the land were departed ; and they carried Manasseh a prisoner to Babylon. At the same time the Assyrian monarch more fully cleared away the remnant of the people left in Israel, and settled additional colonists there. Affliction had a beneficial effect upon the captive king of Judah. " When he was in affliction he besought the Lord his God, and humbled himself greatly before the God of his fathers, and prayed unto him ; and he was intreated of him, and heard his supplication, and brought him again to Jerusalem, into his kingdom. Then Manasseh knew that the Lord he was God." It was better for him to learn this lesson, though by such painful experience, than to perish in ignorance and unbelief. Had he visited Babylon as a prince, and been entertained in its palaces, his idolatry would have been confirmed ; but his confinement in the dungeons of that proud city convinced him of his sin and its folly, and he is recorded as an instance of the willingness of God to accept and welcome returning sinners.

The Assyrian monarch who prevailed against Manasseh, was Esarhaddon ; he had subdued the revolting Babylonians, and reigned till about twelve years after this successful invasion of Judah. The duration of Manasseh's imprisonment is not stated, but he was eventually permitted to return to his kingdom. He endeavoured to undo the evil he had done ; he abolished idolatry, and restored the worship of the Lord, but he was not able thoroughly to remove the evils which he had occasioned, for sacrifices in high places were still continued, and he did not destroy the chief idol he had made. He died and was buried in his own house, which implies that his memory was not publicly honoured. As but few particulars are given of the events which occurred during his long reign, we may believe it was a period, the minute history of which was not profitable to be recorded. We find little more than that Manasseh fortified Jerusalem and garrisoned the frontier towns ; this was rendered necessary from the exposed situation of the country, during the wars be-between Assyria and Egypt, which were now renewed. Some prophets spake to him in the name of the Lord God of Israel, and their words were preserved in the book of the Kings of Israel; see 2 Chron. xxxiii. 18. Whether more was recorded at the time than we read in 2 Kings xxi. 11—15, does not appear; that, how-ever, was enough to show the extent of his evil conduct, and to warn those that came after him.

From the direful effects of the conduct of this mo-narch, Judah never recovered, though a bright gleam of light once more shot across her dark and stormy sky.

A prayer is extant, said to be that of Manasseh when in his affliction; but it is evidently apocryphal, and it is not sanctioned even by the church of Rome. A paraphrase, by a christian poet, represents the repenting monarch as expressing himself in words which will be the language of every truly repenting sinner.

Of boundless mercy I have need,
 My sins, they take deep hold on me,
In number they the grains exceed,
 That form the margin of the sea.

Bow'd with my sense of sin, I faint,
 Beneath the complicated load;
Father, attend my deep complaint,
 I am thy creature, thou my God!

Though I have broke thy righteous law,
 Yet with me let thy Spirit stay;
Thyself from me do not withdraw,
 Nor take my spark of hope away.

In my salvation, Lord, display
 The triumphs of abounding grace;
Tell me my guilt is done away,
 And turn my mourning into praise.

Then shall I add my feeble song
 To their's who chaunt thy praise on high,
And spread, with an immortal tongue,
 Thy glory through the echoing sky.

The simple record of holy writ, already given, is sufficient to inform us that there is mercy even for the chief of sinners. This account was given for the encouragement of the doubting penitent in every succeeding age ; and we may believe that the language of many a saint, who is now in glory, has been,

> My sins are many, like the stars,
>   Or sands upon the shore ;
> But yet the mercies of my God
>   Are infinitely more.

> Manasseh, Paul, and Magdalene,
>   Were pardoned all by thee ;
> I read it, and believe it, Lord,
>   For thou hast pardon'd me !

During this long reign the records of Divine prophecy seem to have been suspended, at least so far as relates to their transmission to future ages. No prophecies now extant are assigned to this period. The harp of prophecy was laid aside, and the martyr's crown exposed to view, and we believe that many rejoiced to wear it—

> They met the tyrant's brandish'd steel,
>   The lion's gory mane,
> They bow'd their necks the death to feel ;
>   Who follows in their train ?

> A noble army—men and boys,
>   The matron and the maid,
> Around the Saviour's throne rejoice,
>   In robes of light array'd.

> They climb'd the steep ascent of heaven,
>   Through peril, toil, and pain
> O God ! to us may grace be given,
>   To follow in their train.

AMON.

REIGNED TWO YEARS.

[B. C. 641—639.]

AMON was the son and the successor of Manasseh. This king was born after his father's return from cap-

tivity, but he followed the early ways of his parent,
and did evil in the sight of the Lord. He turned to
idolatry, and went on from bad to worse, but in two
short years his reign was ended : his ministers and officers conspired against him and slew him, probably
with the view of setting up some usurper, but the people of the land avenged their monarch, the conspirators
were put to death, and his son made king. *Hales*
places at this date the invasion of Judea by the Assyrians under Holofernes, mentioned in the apocryphal or Jewish narrative of Judith, and considers that it
supplies a link in general history. The western states
of Assyria had refused to send auxiliaries to assist Nebuchadnezzar in his war with Media ; after a successful progress in punishing them, the Assyrians approached Judea, but there the general was assassinated
by a Jewess, and the troops, struck with panic fear,
fled, and were pursued by the Israelites. This destruction of the Assyrian army led to a general revolt
among the western nations, while the Medes, uniting
with the Babylonians against the Assyrian empire,
after a warfare of some years, took Nineveh, and the
first universal monarchy was brought to an end. It
may be well here to remark, that in referring to an
apocryphal book, there is no intention to view those
writings in any other light than as ancient histories.
They are not entitled to any of the respect due to the
holy Scriptures, though they may sometimes be advan-
tageously referred to as ancient documents.

JOSIAH.

REIGNED THIRTY-ONE YEARS.

[B. C. 639—608.]

JUDAH, as well as Israel, had now changed its glory
for that which doth not profit. The people had committed two evils ; they had forsaken the Lord, the

P

fountain of living waters, and had hewed them out
cisterns, broken cisterns, that can hold no water.   Out
of the north an evil was about to break forth upon all
the inhabitants of the land ; but a little interval was
granted—a brief opportunity to gather the remaining
wheat into the garner.

Josiah was only eight years old when he succeeded
to the throne of his father, but he was happy in the
care of the high priest Hilkiah, who brought him up
in the nurture and admonition of the Lord.   While
yet young, at the age of sixteen, he gave evident proofs

of piety, and in the twelfth year of his reign he destroyed the images and other appendages of idolatry
throughout Judah.   The account of what was done in
Jerusalem and the vicinity, in this work of reformation,
presents a painful view of the variety and extent to
which idolatry prevailed, and shows the active exertions
of Josiah to render the idols objects of disgust and abhorrence.   Nor were his efforts confined to the two
southern tribes ; six years later, he made a tour through

the central part of Palestine for the same purpose,
which indicates that, in the depressed state of the Assyrian empire, the king of Judah recovered power in
those districts, probably acting as viceroy of the monarch of Assyria.   While thus engaged, or in a later
tour through the country for the same purpose, Josiah
destroyed the altar of Jeroboam at Bethel, according
to the prophecy which had been delivered above 350
years before.   But the nation did not show the same
real desire for reformation as was displayed by the
king.   And now Jeremiah, a youth of one of the families of priests at Anathoth, was commissioned to
declare, in symbolical language, the destruction which
was speedily to come from Assyria.   He felt reluctant to stand forth against the rulers, priests, and people, but was encouraged by the declaration, that the
Lord would be to him as an iron pillar, and as brazen
walls, against all opposers, and they should not prevail
over him.

The eighteenth year of his reign was a busy year
with Josiah.   He caused the temple to be repaired
and fitted for public worship, and while superintending
this work, Hilkiah the high priest found the original
copy of the law, as delivered by Moses, which had
been preserved in the ark, or by its side ; and Josiah's
attention was particularly called to the denunciations
of wrath against the Jewish nation, if they kept not
the precepts of the law.   The king was deeply impressed by these threatenings, and desired inquiry to
be made of the Lord.   Huldah the prophetess confirmed the denunciations against the nation for their
idolatries, but it was promised that Josiah should be gathered to his grave in peace before these evils should be
brought upon Jerusalem.   Upon this the king made a
solemn covenant in the temple, engaging to walk after
the Lord, and to keep his testimonies and statutes ;
and the people pledged themselves to stand to the
same.

The passover was observed in this year with more

solemnity, and a more general attendance, than during any former reign. The king gave nearly forty thousand lambs and kids for passover offerings, besides the larger cattle for burnt sacrifices. This would indicate about half a million of Jews partaking of the passover at Jerusalem, besides others who might provide lambs for themselves. Josiah thus turned to the Lord with his whole heart, and devoted himself to the service of God, in spirit and in truth, but the general conformity of the people seems to have been but outward profession. The bias towards idolatry still remained. Of this they were warned by the prophet Jeremiah, who declared, "though thou wash thee with nitre, and take much sope, yet thine iniquity is marked before me, saith the Lord God."

At the same period Zephaniah denounced judgments against the people : he notices the deceitful professions of " them that worship the host of heaven upon the housetops ; and them that worship and that swear by the Lord, and that swear by Malcham :" thus retaining idolatry while they professed to serve Jehovah, which shows the reluctance many had displayed towards the reformation set forward by the king. The Chemarim, or idolatrous priests, so called from the black garments they wore, in contradistinction, as it were, to the white robes of the priests and Levites, were particularly mentioned as doomed to destruction.

Jeremiah again warned the people of their deceit, especially as to the covenant they made with the Lord. See Jer. xi. and xii. These words were not spoken in private, the prophet was commanded to stand in the gate of the temple, ch. vii., to warn the people who crowded to worship, not to trust in lying words or in a false profession, and to declare that the days approached when the carcases of this people should be meat for the fowls of heaven, and for the beasts of the earth—that the land should be desolate—that the temple should be done unto as Shiloh—that Jerusalem should be heaps, and a den of dragons—and that death should be chosen rather than life by all the residue of them that should remain of this evil family, in the places whither the Lord would drive them. The universal depravity is forcibly stated, ch. v. 1, " Run ye to and fro through the streets of Jerusalem, and see now, and know, and seek in the broad places thereof, if ye can find a man, if there be any that executeth judgment, that seeketh the truth." The prophecies of Jeremiah, chap. iv., v., vi., and also in ch. vii., viii., ix., and x., are particularly impressive, when we consider that they were uttered at a time when the nation professed to be followers of the Lord, and enjoyed a season of rest from their enemies, and even a partial return of wealth and outward prosperity. Thus Habakkuk, who prophesied at the same time, denounced woes against the covetous, which, though primarily denounced against the Assyrian, are applicable to every one " that ladeth himself with thick clay," "whose portion was fat and their meat plenteous."

Jeremiah uttered his prophecies with a deeply sorrowing spirit. How affecting his words,

"Oh that my head were waters,
And mine eyes a fountain of tears,
That I might weep day and night
For the slain of the daughter of my people!
Oh that I had in the wilderness a lodging place of wayfaring men;
That I might leave my people, and go from them!
For they be all adulterers,
An assembly of treacherous men.
And they bend their tongues like their bow for lies:
But they are not valiant for the truth upon the earth;
For they proceed from evil to evil,
And they know not me, saith the Lord.
Take ye heed every one of his neighbour,
And trust ye not in any brother:
For every brother will utterly supplant,
And every neighbour will walk with slanders.
And they will deceive every one his neighbour,
And will not speak the truth:
They have taught their tongue to speak lies,
And weary themselves to commit iniquity.
Thine habitation is in the midst of deceit;
Through deceit they refuse to know me, saith the Lord." Jer. ix. 1—6.

It is not possible to describe the evil of deceit in

stronger language. The prophet showed the proneness of man to deceive himself, and the destructive folly of such conduct. He declared that every one, from the least to the greatest, was given to covetousness, and he gave the earnest warning, not less applicable now than in his day, "Let not the wise man glory in his wisdom," &c. ch. ix. 23, 24. The people did not hear these awful declarations unmoved; the people of Anathoth, Jeremiah's own residence, conspired against him, for which it was declared, no remnant of them should be left. How foolish for men to think they can stop the Divine judgments by silencing God's ministers!

Thirteen years rolled away after the great passover, concerning which time nothing particular is recorded. The prophets continued to warn of approaching judgments, and the people continued their evil ways, till Jeremiah was to declare, in the name of the Lord,

" I have forsaken mine house,
I have left mine heritage;
I have given the dearly beloved of my soul into the hand of her
    enemies.
Mine heritage is unto me as a lion in the forest ;
It crieth out against me:
Therefore have I hated it.
Mine heritage is unto me as a speckled bird,
The birds round about are against her ;
Come ye, assemble all the beasts of the field,
Come to devour.
Many pastors have destroyed my vineyard,
They have trodden my portion under foot,
They have made my pleasant portion a desolate wilderness.
They have made it desolate,
And being desolate it mourneth unto me ;
The whole land is made desolate,
Because no man layeth it to heart." Jer. xii. 7—11.

But a word of mercy still was added.

" And it shall come to pass, after that I have plucked them out,
I will return and have compassion on them, and will bring them
    again,
Every man to his heritage, and every man to his land." Jer. xii. 15.

In the year B.c. 608, Pharaoh-necho, king of Egypt, marched against Assyria, to take advantage of the embarrassed state of that power, by occupying Carchemish;

4

an important pass on the Euphrates. His line of march was through Judea, and Josiah went forth to oppose him, probably thinking it necessary to act in behalf of the Assyrian power, under which the Jewish kingdom had been held since the restoration of Manasseh. Pharaoh counselled Josiah not to interfere in a contest wherein Judah was not concerned, and in which he must make haste. The king of Judah persisted, a battle was fought in the valley of Megiddo, near Mount Tabor. Josiah was wounded mortally: still he died in peace. His death was gain to himself, but loss to his people. Jeremiah lamented this excellent prince, and the people joined in expressing their grief, but not in the words of the Book of the Lamentations of Jeremiah which has come down to us: these were penned after the fall of Jerusalem, to which it refers.

Pharaoh-necho was a powerful prince. He attempted, but without success, to unite the Mediterranean and the Red Sea by a canal ; and failing in this effort, he sent out a fleet, which is said to have sailed round Africa, the voyage occupying three years. The battle with Necho is mentioned by Herodotus, the most ancient of the Greek historians, who describes Jerusalem by the appellation of "the Holy ;" the name given to it by eastern nations at the present day.

JEHOAHAZ.

REIGNED THREE MONTHS.

[B. C. 608.]

THE reign of the second surviving son of Josiah was short, but long enough to show his attachment to idolatry and vice. The cruel ferocity of his temper is delineated by Ezekiel, who describes him as a lion, Ezek. xix. 1—4. But in three months, Pharaoh, returning from his expedition, took Jerusalem, exacted a

heavy contribution, and carried Jehoahaz into Egypt,
where he died, according to the words of Jeremiah.

> " Weep ye not for the dead,
> Neither bemoan him :
> But weep sore for him that goeth away :
> For he shall return no more,
> Nor see his native country.
> For thus saith the Lord
> Touching Shallum the son of Josiah king of Judah,
> Which reigned instead of Josiah his father,
> Which went forth out of his place ;
> He shall not return thither any more :
> But he shall die in the place whither they have led him captive,
> And shall see this land no more." Jer. xxii. 10—12.

The state of dying saints is not to be lamented, but
that of living sinners affords ample ground for sorrow.

JEHOIAKIM.

REIGNED ELEVEN YEARS.

[B. C. 608—597.]

ANOTHER son of Josiah was placed on the throne
by the king of Egypt.   Jehoiakim also did evil in the
sight of the Lord.   But in his first year, Nebuchadnezzar was sent by his father, king Nabopolassar, to reduce
the revolted provinces, when Jehoiakim submitted,
and acknowledged himself his vassal.   The respite
thus obtained was only temporary.   The inspired prophet Jeremiah again foretold approaching evil.

> He saw his people slaves to every lust,
> Lewd, avaricious, arrogant, unjust ;
> He heard the wheels of an avenging God,
> Groan heavily along the distant road ;
> Saw Babylon set wide her two-leav'd brass
> To let the military deluge pass ;
> Jerusalem a prey, her glory soil'd,
> Her princes captive, and her treasures spoil'd ;
> Wept till all Israel heard his bitter cry.—*Cowper.*

The series of prophetic warnings which is found in
Jeremiah : ch. xiii., xiv., xv., xvi., xvii., xviii., should be

referred to, as illustrating the history of this period. Symbolical representations of a linen girdle buried in a hole of a rock, and left that it should rot, and of bottles filled with wine, gave warning of the destruction to come. The judgments upon the royal family of Judah were especially noticed.

"Hear ye, and give ear ; be not proud :
For the Lord hath spoken.
Give glory to the Lord your God,
Before he cause darkness,
And before your feet stumble upon the dark mountains,
And, while ye look for light,
He turn it into the shadow of death, and make it gross darkness.
But if ye will not hear it,
My soul shall weep in secret places for your pride ;
And mine eye shall weep sore, and run down with tears,
Because the Lord's flock is carried away captive.
Say unto the king and to the queen,
Humble yourselves, sit down :
For your principalities shall come down,
Even the crown of your glory.
The cities of the south shall be shut up,
And none shall open them :
Judah shall be carried away captive, all of it,
It shall be wholly carried away captive.
Lift up your eyes, and behold them that come from the north."
　　　　　　　　　　　　　　　　　　Jer. xiii. 15—20.

A very emphatic inquiry, showing their neglect of the people entrusted to their charge is added, " Where is the flock that was given thee, thy beautiful flock ? "

A famine and drought were sent as precursors of severer judgments. These inflictions were predicted by Jeremiah, till his repeated solemn warnings rendered him an object of dislike to the rulers and people in general. Faithful ministers in every age have experienced this, but probably none more than Jeremiah. His anguish of soul forcibly expressed.

"Woe is me ! my mother,
That thou hast borne me a man of strife
And a man of contention to the whole earth !
I have neither lent on usury, nor men have lent to me on usury ;
Yet every one of them doth curse me." Jer. xv. 10.

The promise of the Lord given in answer was plain and encouraging ; still the prophet continued to plead in the bitterness of his soul.

" O Lord, thou knowest: remember me,
Aud visit me, and revenge me of my persecutors;
Take me not away in thy longsuffering:
Know that for thy sake I have suffered rebuke.
Thy words were found, and I did eat them;
And thy word was unto me the joy and rejoicing of mine heart:
For I am called by thy name, O Lord God of hosts.
I sat not in the assembly of the mockers, nor rejoiced;
I sat alone because of thy hand:
For thou hast filled me with indignation.
Why is my pain perpetual,
And my wound incurable, which refuseth to be healed?
Wilt thou be altogether unto me as a liar,
And as waters that fail?"   Jer. xv. 15—18.

Again the Lord mercifully supported Jeremiah with
a direct assurance that he should be preserved.

" And I will make thee unto this people a fenced brazen wall:
And they shall fight against thee, but they shall not prevail against thee:
For I am with thee to save thee
And to deliver thee, saith the Lord.
And I will deliver thee out of the hand of the wicked,
And I will redeem thee out of the hand of the terrible." Jer. xv. 20, 21.

New strength was imparted to him, and he went
forth, again telling of the judgments at hand, minutely
describing them.   Here we find him pointing out the
source of all the evil doings he was directed to reprove.

" The heart is deceitful above all things,
And desperately wicked: who can know it?"

The chapters from xiv. to xvii. inclusive, are particularly impressive when minutely examined.   In the last
of these we find that the breach of the sabbath was
expressly pointed out as a national sin, and its due observance required, by the prophet, who stood in the
gates of Jerusalem, the chief places of concourse, and
openly declared that if the sabbath was not hallowed,
a fire should be kindled in those thoroughfares, which
should destroy the palaces of the city.   The absolute
and almighty power of the Most High was shown
under the type of the potter turning the clay in his
hand, according to his will; and the perversion of that
truth, by the people declaring that then there was no
hope, but that they would walk after their own devices,

is noticed. Chap. xix. contains a solemn exhortation delivered before the elders of the people, and of the priests, assembled for the purpose at the head of the valley of Hinnom, and in the court of the temple.

Pashur, the ruler of the temple, smote the prophet, placed him in confinement, and exposed him to public scorn; for which, and for his false prophecies, he was personally warned of his captivity and death at Babylon. In ch. xxii. we find the prophet standing before the king, and declaring the disgraceful end which awaited Jehoiakim, that he should be buried with the burial of an ass, drawn and cast forth beyond the gates of Jerusalem. And again the people were publicly told, see ch. xxvi., that the city should be desolate, and

without an inhabitant; upon which the holy prophet
was threatened with death, and was carried before the
council of princes and priests. Some ventured to
plead for him, alleging that Micah had spoken as
strongly, but king Hezekiah and the people had hearkened unto him, and the evil was deferred. Upon this
Jeremiah was spared, though he stood his ground,
while Urijah, another prophet, who fled for fear, was
brought from Egypt, and was put to death. Ahikam,
one of the rulers, was raised up as a protector for the
faithful prophet.

In Jeremiah, ch. xlvi., there is mention of another
Egyptian expedition against Carchemish, and Jehoiakim was encouraged thereby to revolt; but Nebuchadnezzar defeated the Egyptians near the Euphrates, and
their king came no more out of his own land.

Nebuchadnezzar now prepared to chastise Jehoiakim, and the general consternation which prevailed is
shown by the Rechabites taking refuge in Jerusalem,
Jer. xxxv. Their obedience is contrasted with the disobedience of the Jewish nation. It was declared that
Jonadab, the son of Rechab, should not want a man
to stand before the Lord for ever; and his posterity
exist in the east as a distinctly recognised people, even
at the present day.

Destruction was nigh at hand, and the prophet was
commissioned to speak yet more plainly. In Jer. xxv.
it is expressly stated, " This whole land shall be a desolation, and an astonishment; and these nations shall
serve the king of Babylon seventy years." In the same
chapter the troubles coming upon all the nations around
are distinctly set forth in figurative language, which
probably was accompanied by some symbolical action
of the prophet. Nor were the declarations of the
prophet only to be expressed by him in words. Jeremiah being under some restraint, which prevented him
from entering the temple, or publicly exercising the
ministerial office, Baruch was commanded to write the

words of the Lord in a book, and to read them publicly
in the temple, on the great fast of the day of expiation,

when people had assembled from all parts of the land.
Baruch was appointed to this office, but a word was
given, personally addressed to him, which contains important advice to all who are called to discharge similar duties, lest they should be unduly affected, by
being thus employed.   " Seekest thou great things for
thyself? seek them not: for, behold, I will bring evil
upon all flesh, saith the Lord."   Yet a word of encouragement was added, " but thy life will I give unto
thee for a prey in all places whither thou goest."

In the fourth year of Jehoiakim, Nebuchadnezzar
advanced towards Egypt, subduing all the northern
conquests of Pharaoh, and besieged and took Jerusalem.   He carried away some of the sacred vessels,
and placed them in the temple of Belus, at Babylon ;
and also some of the princes and nobles were removed
as captives, among whom was Daniel and his companions.   See Daniel i. 1—7.   This may be considered

Q

as the beginning of the Babylonish captivity, B.C. 605,
which, according to the prophetic warning of Jeremiah,
was to continue seventy years. Nebuchadnezzar was
recalled from this expedition by the death of his father,
upon which he hastened to take possession of the supreme power.

Jehoiakim submitted, and was left to reign as a vassal of Babylon. In the following year a fast was proclaimed, when Baruch again read the roll. This fast
was instituted to commemorate the recent taking of
Jerusalem, and is still observed by the Jews. The contents of the roll now attracted the attention of the
princes; they carried it to the king, who after hearing

a small part, cut the roll to pieces, and burned it in the
fire upon the hearth which stood before him. The remembrance of this act of impiety is still preserved by
the Jews, who keep an annual fast for the burning of
Jeremiah's prophetic roll. Orders were given to seize
the prophet and his scribe, but " the Lord hid them."
They were protected from the wrath of the king, and

an express declaration was made of the judgment
about to come upon him personally.

" Therefore thus saith the Lord of Jehoiakim king of Judah ;
He shall have none to sit upon the throne of David :
And his dead body shall be cast out
In the day to the heat,
And in the night to the frost.
And I will punish him and his seed and his servants
For their iniquity ;
And I will bring upon them,
And upon the inhabitants of Jerusalem, and upon the men of Judah,
All the evil that I have pronounced against them ;
But they hearkened not." Jer. xxxvi. 30, 31.

Jehoiakim despised this warning, and rebelled
against Nebuchadnezzar, who being engaged against
the Medes and Lydians, sent orders to the vassal nations
round Judea, to ravage and plunder the land.   They
did so for three years, when in the eleventh year of this
wicked king they surrounded Jerusalem, and Jehoiakim,
being taken prisoner, was brought to Nebuchadnezzar,
who intended to carry him in chains to Babylon, but
he died, and his dead body was cast out unburied,
agreeably to the word of the prophet. *Prideaux* considers that he was slain by the confederate forces, and
his body left to decay without burial.

JEHOIACHIN.

REIGNED THREE MONTHS.

[B. C. 597.]

JEHOIACHIN did not take warning from his father's
fate ; the predatory bands still blockaded Jerusalem,
and he did evil, so as to bring upon himself the express
declaration of judgment, Jer. xxii., xxiii., that none of
his descendants should prosper, or sit upon the throne.
Here again we may notice, how denunciations of wrath
are mixed with declarations of mercy.   This prophecy
contains also a clear statement concerning the promised

Messiah, and a warning against false prophets. After three months, Nebuchadnezzar arrived before Jerusalem, when finding that the city could not be defended, Jehoiachin surrendered, and was carried captive to Babylon, where he remained a close prisoner till the death of Nebuchadnezzar, nearly forty years.

The king of Babylon took decisive measures for weakening the Jewish power; seventeen thousand persons, the most eminent for rank and abilities, whether as statesmen, warriors, or craftsmen, were removed to Babylon, with the wealth of the nation; those who remained were chiefly the poorest sort of the people of the land. Among the captives was Ezekiel, who with others was placed at the river Chebar; Mordecai also was taken to Babylon at this time.

ZEDEKIAH.

REIGNED ELEVEN YEARS.

[B. C. 597—586.]

THE brother of Jehoiachin was placed on the throne, and his name changed from Mattaniah to Zedekiah. He followed the same evil courses, and pursued the same disastrous policy as his predecessors. Notwithstanding the precise fulfilment of Jeremiah's prophecies, the words of the prophet were still despised, but he continued to utter them. In ch. xxiv., under the type of good and bad figs, was shown the different manner of the Lord's dealings with those who were led into captivity, and those who were suffered to remain in the land. The sufferings of the former would be for their good, while the latter would not take warning, but would fill up the measure of their iniquities till they were consumed.

In ch. xxix. is a letter sent by the prophet to the Jews at Babylon, stating the precise number of years the

captivity would last, namely, till seventy years should
be accomplished, also counselling them to act with
propriety in the land where they were, and to seek its
welfare ; advice which it is well for all to keep in
mind, and to act upon, wherever they are placed in
this changing world.   To this was added a distinct
promise of the restoration of the Jews, in ch. xxx., xxxi.,
with a notice of the new covenant, ver. 31—34,
beautifully referring to the first settlement of the Jews
in the land of promise, adding a statement of glorious times for Jerusalem, which seems to belong to
prophecy yet unfulfilled, for it cannot be said of Jerusalem when rebuilt after the Babylonish captivity, that it
was holy to the Lord, not plucked up nor thrown down
again.

From Jeremiah xxix. it appears, that in the agitated
state of Jerusalem, false prophets abounded, and that
some were punished even by the enemy ; and that the
true prophets were threatened by these impostors.
From ch. xxvii., which properly belongs to the reign of
Zedekiah, we find that several neighbouring kings
sought to excite the king of Judah to join them in a
revolt against Babylon ; but the prophet, by the sign
of a yoke placed upon his own neck, warned those
powers to submit to Nebuchadnezzar.   Hananiah, a
false prophet, opposed Jeremiah, and sought to promote
this revolt, declaring that in two years the captives
should be brought back ; for which he was rebuked,
and his own death denounced : and it is recorded that
he died two months afterwards.   The wickedness which
then prevailed at Jerusalem is described by Ezekiel
ch. viii.   That prophet, a captive beyond Babylon,
was carried in the spirit to Jerusalem, and in a vision
had set before him the idol erected in the temple, and
saw the elders and princes engaged in the idolatrous
and abominable secret mysteries of the Egyptians,
Phenicians, and Persians.   The awful consequence,
" Therefore will I deal in fury : mine eye shall not
spare, neither will I have pity : and though they cry

Q 2

in mine ears with a loud voice, yet will I not hear them,"
was declared to the prophet. Were the secret abominations practised in any of our own cities set before us,
we might, like the prophet, justly fear that destruction
would be brought upon all the inhabitants.

The judgments to come on the surrounding nations
were expressly declared; see Jeremiah xlviii., xlix.;
and on Zedekiah going to Babylon, as a tributary
monarch, having had at that time the wisdom to refuse
to revolt, Jeremiah sent an animated and express prophecy of the fall of Babylon, ch. l., li., which, while
it referred particularly to that ancient enemy of the
people of God, doubtless has reference to other foes of
later date, to whom the same name of "Babylon" is
applied in Scripture. The description of the return
from captivity is very beautiful.

> "In those days, and in that time, saith the Lord,
> The children of Israel shall come,
> They and the children of Judah together,
> Going and weeping:
> They shall go, and seek the Lord their God.
> They shall ask the way to Zion
> With their faces thitherward, saying,
> Come, and let us join ourselves to the Lord
> In a perpetual covenant that shall not be forgotten." Jer. l. 4, 5.

Ezekiel, at Babylon, gave similar warnings.

The national sins continued to increase. From
Jeremiah and Ezekiel it is evident that idolatry had
been practised worse than ever, the king and the people
were given up to their own devices. This is noted in
2 Chron. xxxvi. 14—17. In the ninth year of Zedekiah, that king formed an alliance with Egypt, upon
which Nebuchadnezzar invaded the land. Directed by
the divination of arrows, the conqueror left Ammon for
a time, and again besieged Jerusalem. Jeremiah was
then at liberty, when Zedekiah sent to request his
prayers, and of course looked for some declaration of
what was to come to pass. Jeremiah plainly declared
the fate which awaited the king, and the destruction to
come upon Jerusalem; ch. xxxiv. 1—6. This led
to the arrest and imprisonment of the prophet, but the

king and the people, humbled by the sense of their
danger, proclaimed that their brethren, whom they had
retained as slaves, without regard to the Divine law,
should be allowed to go free.   Jeremiah was now confined in the prison-court of the palace, where he was
directed to repeat his denunciation of the fate which
awaited Zedekiah, and to give a sign of the future deliverance of the nation, although then reduced to extremity, by purchasing some ground at Anathoth belonging to his uncle.   The approaching destruction of Jerusalem was again distinctly foretold, and a promise of
the Messiah connected with the message of woe.

" In those days, and at that time,
Will I cause the Branch of righteousness to grow up unto David ;
And he shall execute judgment and righteousness in the land.
In those days shall Judah be saved,
And Jerusalem shall dwell safely:
And this is the name wherewith she shall be called,
The Lord our Righteousness." Jer. xxxiii. 15, 16.

After some months, an army of Egyptians advanced
to the relief of Jerusalem ; the Chaldean army broke
up the siege, and proceeded to repel them, upon which
the Egyptians retired.   This partial deliverance induced the Jews to show the hollowness of their repentance ; they again enslaved their brethren, whom they
had let go free.   Jeremiah, who had been liberated,
strongly censured this wickedness, and declared that
the Chaldean army would come again, and burn the
city.   After this he endeavoured to leave the city, but
was apprehended at the gate, and falsely charged with
an intention to desert to the enemy, upon which the
princes caused him to be put into a dungeon, in the
house of the secretary ; for then, as now in the east,
it was common for men of rank to have places for cus-
tody in their palaces.   Zedekiah, however, sent for the
prophet, and inquired concerning the Divine will, when
he was told that he should be delivered to the king of
Babylon ; but at Jeremiah's request, he kept the prophet as a prisoner in the palace court.   He ordered
Jeremiah to be supplied with a daily allowance of

bread, which already began to be scarce, as a famine
was approaching.

The prophet, continuing to declare the approaching
capture of the city, and that those who remained there
should perish, while those who went out to the enemy
and surrendered themselves should be spared, the
princes urged that the prophet should be put to death,
alleging that he discouraged the people. Jeremiah was
then thrown into a noisome dungeon of one of the ruler's

palaces, a large and deep pit with mire at the bottom.
Here he would soon have perished but for the kindness of Ebed-melech, a black eunuch, one of the royal
attendants, who obtained the king's authority to draw
up the prophet, and replace him in the prison-court.

Zedekiah again sent for Jeremiah, who counselled

him to go forth and surrender himself to the Chaldeans, with an assurance that if he would do so, the
city should be spared ; but false shame and fear prevented the Jewish king from following this advice, and
the siege was again formed, in the eleventh year of
that prince. All these events were made known to
Ezekiel in the land of Chaldea, by visions and other
Divine communications.

Famine and its disastrous consequences prevailed in
Jerusalem, as described by Jeremiah in his Lamentations ; the children and sucklings swooned in the
streets of the city, saying to their mothers, " Where is
corn and wine ?" The young children fainted for
hunger in the top of every street ; the young and the
old lay on the ground in the streets, and women even
ate the infants they had swaddled with their hands.
All the horrors which have been exhibited in times of
dearth, before and since, appear to have taken place

in Jerusalem at this time. At last, at midnight, on the
ninth day of the fourth month, the besiegers stormed

the city, and put many of the inhabitants to the sword,
even in the temple courts.   These dreadful scenes are
described by Jeremiah in the Lamentations.

Zedekiah, and his courtiers and officers, fled by a
postern gate ; but, after escaping through the hilly
country, they were overtaken in the plains of Jericho,
and carried prisoners to Nebuchadnezzar, then at
Riblah.   The captive king was upbraided for his in-
gratitude and rebellion, his eyes were then put out,
the last painful scene he was suffered to behold being
the slaughter of his own sons ; after this he was carried to Babylon, where he died.   Thus, notwithstanding the apparent contradiction in the prophecies of
Ezekiel and Jeremiah, respecting Zedekiah, both were
fulfilled.   The latter declared, Jer. xxxii. 4, 5, xxxiv.
3—5, that Zedekiah should be taken prisoner, should
see the king of Babylon, should be carried captive to
Babylon, and die there in peace.   Ezekiel, xii. 13, had
declared that the Jewish monarch should be brought
captive to Babylon, but should not see it.   The Jewish
tradition is, that this apparent contradiction between
the words of the two prophets, induced the king to reject the warning of both.   How often do we see men
actuated by a similar principle, of being wise above
what is written, rejecting the word of God, because
they fancy that some portions of it contradict others.
Let us beware that we sin not thus to our own destruction.   The Jewish rabbins state that the captive Hebrews exclaimed at his burial, " Alas ! king Zedekiah
is dead, who has drank up the dregs of all ages, who
has suffered the punishment due to all his predecessors."   It is true that the cup of Israel's iniquity
was now full ; but let us never forget, that every one
is punished for his own guilt, even though the sins of
his forefathers may appear to rest upon his head.

In less than a month from the capture of Jerusalem,
Nebuchadnezzar sent orders for the demolition of the
city and temple of Jerusalem ; the buildings were
burned or levelled with the ground, and all the wealth

and property destroyed or carried away, as well as all the surviving inhabitants, except a few of the poorest.

The awful scene exhibited by the ruins of this glorious city, is delineated by the psalmist Asaph, Psa. lxxix.; and the ravages of the destroyer casting fire into the sanctuary, and breaking down the carved work with axes and hammers, is described in Psa. lxxiv. while Psa. lxxiii. enumerates the enemies of Judah, and declares their fate, and Psa. xciv. probably was written to console the church under its sufferings.

Thus the city of Jerusalem and the temple were laid in ruins, four hundred and seventy years after the erection of the latter glorious building by Solomon. Though Nebuzar-adan thus destroyed the temple, and burned the dwellings of Jerusalem, and carried away captive many of the people, his purpose was not utterly to devastate the land. The design of the king of Babylon, doubtless was, that it should be retained as a province of his empire. Colonies were already planted in the district of the ten tribes ; in Judea, for the present, certain of the poor of the land were left for vine dressers and for husbandmen, and to them vineyards and fields were assigned. Gedaliah, the son of Ahikam, was appointed to be the ruler. Jeremiah, the prophet, at the special command of Nebuchadnezzar, who caused him to be brought before him at Rámah, was committed to the care of Nebuzar-adan. The Babylonian general referred to the true cause of these judgments upon Jerusalem, namely, because the Jews had sinned against the Lord, and had not obeyed his voice. He also recommended the prophet to go to Gedaliah, and remain with him, unless he felt it a duty to proceed elsewhere. Ahikam, the father of the governor, was a person of rank and influence ; he is noticed, 2 Kings xxii. 12, as employed to inquire of the prophetess respecting the denunciations contained in the law, the copy of which was found in the temple and brought to Josiah ; and, in Jeremiah xxvi. 24, we find him protecting the prophet from the rage of

Jehoiakim and the excited feelings of the people, which
shows that he possessed considerable influence, and
his son Gedaliah evidently was popular, and of an
excellent character.

Many of the Jewish captains, and people also, had
escaped when Jerusalem was taken, and were roving
in the deserted and secluded parts of the land. When
these men heard that their conqueror allowed some of
their nation to remain, and had even appointed one of
their own leaders to be governor, they went to Gedaliah, who fixed his residence at Mizpah, and were encouraged by him to profess themselves ready to serve
the king of Babylon, and to dwell in various parts of
the country. Many of the Jews who had fled to
Moab, and Edom, and other neighbouring countries,
also availed themselves of this arrangement. As the
time of harvest was past, and that of the vintage had
arrived, the greater part of those who were willing to
accept the king of Babylon's mercy, dispersed themselves through the forsaken parts of the country, col-
lecting a part of the rich products of the earth, which
were spoiling for want of hands to gather them.

The dispersion of the Jews was to be yet more
complete, and that by their own acts. Ishmael, the
son of Nethaniah, one of the royal family, thought he
could make himself ruler over the land now that the
Babylonians were gone. He was encouraged to this
by Baalis, king of Ammon. Gedaliah, though warned
of his danger, was unwilling to think evil of one of
those who like himself had so lately escaped the
Divine judgments, and he refused to allow Ishmael to
be cut off secretly. This refusal was right ; we are
not justified in doing evil that good may come ; but
he would have done well to have been on his guard
against treachery, yet it seems that he could not rely
on the report of one who had expressed himself desirous to commit a murder.

Ishmael and his companions came to Mizpah in the
seventh month, when most of the people were busily

engaged in gathering the fruits of the land. He was
received in a friendly manner by Gedaliah, but treach-
erously slew him at an entertainment provided by the
unsuspicious chief.   Ishmael also massacred many
adherents of Gedaliah, whether Jews or Babylonians.
The day following, he heard of the approach of eighty
men who were on their way to the ruins of the temple
with offerings, and having met them at the entrance of
Mizpah, falsely pretended a wish to present them to
Gedaliah, and hypocritically expressed himself ready
to join in their lamentations. But he caused them
also to be massacred, excepting ten, who having stores
of wheat, barley, oil, and honey concealed in pits, as
it is still customary to store grain in the east, were
spared, doubtless on condition of giving up their
wealth to the followers of Ishmael. The bodies of
the victims were cast into a large excavation made
by king Asa, during his wars with Israel, for defence
or for a place of concealment, or more probably for a
reservoir of water.

Ishmael, though thus successful, felt himself insecure. He took those whom he had spared, including
the daughters of king Zedekiah, and began his retreat
to Ammon, but was overtaken at Gibeon by Johanan
and other captains, who had been absent from Mizpah.
The prisoners, and those who followed Ishmael unwillingly, rejoiced at their deliverance, and the murderer
escaped with eight attendants only. This treachery
and destruction brought additional calamities to the
humbled people of Israel, which have been ever since
commemorated by a fast.

Johanan, and those who remained, soon resolved
upon the course they would pursue. They were apprehensive that the king of Babylon would consider
them as guilty of the murder of Gedaliah, whom he
had appointed their ruler, and therefore they retired
beyond Jerusalem, thinking to go into Egypt. But
while at Chimham, near Bethlehem, they resorted to
Jeremiah, and asked him to seek direction for them

R

from the Lord, although they had already resolved on their proceedings. He undertook to pray for them, and after ten days an answer was vouchsafed, expressly telling them not to fear the king of Babylon, but to remain in Judea, and warning them that if they went to Egypt, they should suffer from the judgments they thought to avoid ; the sword, famine, and pestilence should overtake all those of them who sojourned in Egypt. But this plain and express declaration was despised. As the prophet told them, they dissembled in their hearts, and had resolved on the course they would pursue, before they asked for direction. Johanan and his companions were determined to go to Egypt, and they compelled all who were with them to proceed into that land, whither many of their nation had already gone. They came to Tahpanhes, or Daphne, where they were permitted to reside.

Jeremiah was thus carried to Egypt, but he did not hesitate to declare the word of the Lord, and expressly gave warning that Nebuchadnezzar would come to that very place, and set up a throne upon some stones which he collected, and that this conqueror would ravage Egypt, and destroy its false gods. He reminded the Jews throughout the country of their idolatries in Palestine, and of the repeated warnings given them as to the certain destruction which would follow. Here the tenderness of the Lord towards them, is beautifully expressed by the use of terms applicable to human passions and feelings ; " I sent unto you all my servants the prophets, rising early and sending them, saying, Oh, do not this abominable thing that I hate." Jeremiah declared to the Jews who were in the land, that as they had been induced to worship the deities of Egypt, they should be consumed and fall there. His countrymen avowed their idolatry, and refused to hearken to the words of the Lord. Both men and women declared with unblushing effrontery, that they would not hearken to what the prophet had spoken in the name of Jehovah! They even ascribed their present misfortunes to the want of a due observance of idolatrous rites !

The prophet hesitated not again to denounce the sure consequences of this conduct, and that only a small number should be permitted to return into the land of Judah, who might testify of the fulfilment of the Divine word. With this solemn warning the history of the remnant who escaped from Jerusalem, and were not carried captive to Babylon, is closed. It is a tradition of the Jews, that the prophet Jeremiah was stoned to death by these idolaters, who refused to listen to the word of the Lord.

From general history we learn that these predictions of Jeremiah were fulfilled very soon afterwards. Nebuchadnezzar having taken Tyre, and being disappointed of the pillage he had expected, the inhabitants escaping by sea with their wealth, resolved to gratify his army with the spoils of Egypt. This was explicitly foretold by the prophet Ezekiel.

> " Son of man! Nebuchadrezzar king of Babylon caused his army
> To serve a great service against Tyrus;
> Every head was made bald, and every shoulder was peeled :
> Yet had he no wages, nor his army, for Tyrus,
> For the service that he had served against it ;
> Therefore thus saith the Lord God :
> Behold ! I will give the land of Egypt
> Unto Nebuchadrezzar king of Babylon ;
> And he shall take her multitude,
> And take her spoil, and take her prey
> And it shall be the wages for his army.
> I have given him the land of Egypt
> For his labour wherewith he served against it,
> Because they wrought for me, saith the Lord God."
>   Ezek. xxix. 18—20.

At that time Egypt was weakened by domestic feuds, and offered little resistance to the invader. It was ravaged throughout its whole extent, and so completely desolated, that it did not recover for forty years. Nebuchadnezzar left Amasis as his deputy ; and Apries, or Pharaoh-hophra as he is called in Scripture, soon after attempting to recover the kingdom, was taken prisoner and put to death, exactly as foretold by Jeremiah, xliv. 30. Most of the Jews residing in Egypt were taken by the invaders; some were slain, and others carried to Babylon; only a small number escaped. These events were minutely prophesied by Ezekiel. See ch. xxix.—xxxii.

Jeremiah, when thus explicitly declaring the destruction of the idolatrous Jews and the desolating judgments about to come upon Egypt, was to record God's promises of mercy towards Israel.

" Fear thou not, O Jacob my servant !
Saith the Lord : for I am with thee ;
For I will make a full end of all the nations
Whither I have driven thee :
But I will not make a full end of thee,
But correct thee in measure ;
Yet will I not leave thee wholly unpunished." Jer. xlvi. 28.

The fulfilment of this prophecy is witnessed to the present day. Where now is Babylon or Thebes, where can the Chaldeans, or the ancient Egyptians be traced? To the final accomplishment we are still to look forward. ,The Jewish people are indeed a standing miracle; nothing but the especial interference of Divine power could have kept them in a distinct and

separate state, under every untoward disadvantage
as to their government and religion. Thus it is a
most remarkable miracle that a full end has not been
made of them.

THE DESTRUCTION OF JERUSALEM.

Jeremiah xix. xxxii.

Fallen is thy throne, O Israel!
Silence is on thy plains.
Thy dwellings all lie desolate;
Thy children weep in chains.
Where are the dews that fed thee
On Etham's barren shore?
That fire from heaven which led thee,
Now lights thy path no more!

Lord, thou didst love Jerusalem!
Once she was all thine own;
Her love thy fairest heritage,
Her power thy glory's throne.
Till evil came and blighted
Thy long-lov'd olive tree,
And Salem's shrines were lighted
For other gods than thee.

Then sank the star of Solyma;
Then passed her glory's day;
Like heath that in the wilderness
The wild wind whirls away.
Silent and waste her bowers
Where once the mighty trod,
And sunk those guilty towers
Where Baal reigned as God.

" Go," said the Lord, " ye conquerors!
Steep in her blood your swords;
And raze to earth her battlements,
For th· y are not the Lord's;
Tell Zion's mournful daughter,
O'er kindred bones she'll tread;
And Hinnom's hall of slaughter
Shall hide but half her dead."

But soon shall other pictur'd scenes
In brighter visions rise,
When Zion's sun shall sevenfold shine
O'er all her mourners' eyes;
And on her mountains beauteous stand
The messengers of peace;
" Salvation by the Lord's right hand!"
They shout, and never cease.

In the preceding brief delineation of the concluding reigns of the kings of Israel and Judah, the attention of the reader has been directed to the light thrown upon the historical details, by the writings of the prophets ; and those of Isaiah and Jeremiah supply ample materials for the purpose, and have been noticed, although in an imperfect manner. The method by which the Divine will was communicated to these holy men, appears principally to have been by a Divine impulse, enabling or urging the prophet to speak forcibly and freely on matters then engaging or claiming attention, whether sacred or civil. Sometimes visions or revelations were made in a trance, or state of ecstasy, during which symbolic representations or graphic ideas were presented to the prophet's mind, or an outline of future events passed before his mental view, as in distant prospect. This latter method seems frequently to have been pursued, when the restoration of Israel or the coming of the Messiah, were the principal subjects. As a spectator standing on an ascent in a mountainous country beholds " Alps o'er Alps arise," and loses sight of the valleys and glens between, while he contemplates the objects which occupy the distant eminences, so the mind of the prophet glanced as it were from height to height. The approaching deliverance of Israel was soon absorbed in the bright but distant outlines of its latter-day glory ; and the peaceful triumphs of the first coming of Christ, as the Saviour of his people, were absorbed by the dazzling radiance of his second coming, as King of kings and Lord of lords —Christ suffering was united with Christ triumphant ; and thus the great features of the future dispensation were impressed upon the mind of the prophet, without any distinct idea being given of the space of time and the crowd of events, intervening between the glorious though differing manifestations.

These remarks may be considered as particularly

applicable .to the revelations respecting the Saviour, communicated by Isaiah; but one remarkable illustration may be pointed out in the prophet Habakkuk, ch. iii. He appears to behold the crying iniquities of his country, and then to see the Chaldeans, " that bitter and hasty nation," their horsemen spreading themselves over the land, swifter than leopards, more fierce than wolves, and like eagles hastening to their prey; scoffing at kings, scorning the princes, and deriding the strong holds—" come all for violence," ravaging and spoiling the land, and ransacking the hoards of the covetous oppressor, while shame and disgrace overwhelm the idolater. " The Lord is in his holy temple, let all the earth keep silence before him!"   But a still more powerful inspiration follows. The interval of ages is lost ; the Lord appears in glorious majesty, as from Sinai of old. Dread and fear come upon the enemies of his truth. The prophet beholds a country inhabited as in his own time ; not only are the tents and habitations agitated by preparation for removal at the approach of an invader, which shortly was realized in the land—but even nature itself is troubled and disturbed when the Lord marches through the land in indignation. The prophet sees this destruction poured forth upon the wicked, while the Divine power is manifested as possessed and displayed by the Saviour, who once was despised and rejected of men. The prophet trembles, but there is rest for the followers of the Lord in the day of trouble, and in this view he is enabled to look above all earthly afflictions and privations, while he rejoices in the Lord, and joys in the God of his salvation.

When considering the period from the accession of David to the Babylonish captivity, as containing much that is instructive matter of history, let us not forget that it is especially important, since a large portion of the Bible, nearly the whole of the Old Testament, from 2 Samuel to Zephaniah, originated in these four centuries, and was committed to writing during this space of four hundred years. How precious this treasure, especially since the revelations of Christ therein contained, are so much clearer than those of the preceding three thousand years! We see the whole of these prophetic revelations pointing to one Personage of the highest dignity, and proclaiming the accomplishment of one purpose, the most merciful that can be conceived of an all-merciful Being. Is not, it has well been asked—is not the object of this scheme, the Lamb of God that taketh away the sin of the world, worthy of all the honour thus reflected upon him? And as to the lengthened chain of circumstances by which events were carried forward with this great end in view, remember—

> God moves in a mysterious way,
> 　His wonders to perform
> He plants his footsteps in the sea,
> 　And rides upon the storm.
>
> Deep in unfathomable mines
> 　Of never-failing skill,
> He treasures up his bright designs,
> 　And works his sovereign will.
>
> Blind unbelief is sure to err,
> 　And scan his work in vain :
> God is his own interpreter,
> 　And he will make it plain.

J. Hill, Printer, Black Horse Court, Fleet Street, London.

Printed in the USA
CPSIA information can be obtained
at www.ICGtesting.com
LVHW052342101023
760585LV00013B/803

9 781166 168476